The Enigma of Creation

ISBN: 978-1-387-76299-6

Table of Contents

List of Tables

Preface

This work represents a personal, theological journey, which took place over the course of several years. My ideas and conclusions were not first formed, at once, and simply written down. Rather, as all the pieces were slowly laid out, an approach began to take shape and was refined.

The goal of this work is not dogma. And yet the evidence is presented in such a way, so that all of it can be accounted for in any conclusions which the reader may reach. Of course, I offer my own conclusions for consideration. Ultimately, the goal of this work is only to encourage a deeper and more sensitive approach to the creation text of Genesis 1. To that end, I pray that this work strengthens your faith in God, and His Son, as much as it has mine.

Rick Brower

Introduction

In recent years, few topics have generated more interest and prompted more debate across the broad spectrum of Christian denominations, than that of the Biblical creation texts. And in particular, the text of Genesis 1 has played a controversial role. It is often assumed that this creation passage is plainly understood without any interpretive effort. However, it is the intent of this work to demonstrate that such an assumption is entirely incorrect. This may come as a surprise to those who have not thoroughly studied both the passage and its history. And so, a review of the facts must be in order.

If we simply open the Bible at random, and presuppose that the words on the page are meant to be taken at face value, we may very well experience a positive and uplifting result, albeit in an elementary fashion. And yet, this is not the only way to study the Bible; it does not hold true in every case. For better or for worse, this method simply ignores several important aspects of Scripture, such as the original language of the text, as well as the original audience and culture to whom it was written. In some cases, this method may even overlook information which is elsewhere supplied, and disagreements over Biblical interpretation abound. Regarding Genesis 1, the evidence overwhelmingly demands that we abandon such a naïve perspective. Genesis 1 is certainly not straight forward, nor has it *ever* been so. The text is not easily understood.

In fact, Genesis 1 has consistently proven itself to be an enigma of Biblical proportion.[1] Thus the apparent modern regard, particularly amongst fundamentalist groups, for the so called 'literal' view of Genesis 1 is of grave concern. Author and public lecturer Paul Marston notes, 'In popular culture it is generally imagined that until recently most Christians 'took Genesis literally' and that only post-Darwin have some more 'liberal' theologians sought to 'compromise' by trying to symbolize it all away. But this is

---

[1]See Appendix I. The Enigma of Creation

demonstrably false.'[2] We cannot even agree on what that plain, literal reading was in all points.[3]

How is it that so many Bible commentators have struggled to make the apparent details of creation fit into their world view? And why is it that so many different interpretations have been proposed for the same set of physical problems? Indeed, it seems much easier for us to uncover all the conundrums, discontinuities, and apparent absurdities in the literal creation text, with respect to the physical world, than it is to resolve these in harmony with the rest of the Bible, the spiritual world. With so many options to choose from, it is no wonder that the text of Genesis 1 has been the focus of the most protracted theological controversy of all time.

It is assumed that all Christians would immediately agree that Genesis 1 teaches spiritual principles. It is not assumed that all Christians can actually define those principles, nor do they grasp the implications of those principles. So then let us state the premise of this work in another way. Scripture itself teaches us that the plain literal text in question is bound by the nonliteral, or spiritual, meaning which it also must convey. By temporarily laying aside the literal uncertainties of Genesis 1, and focusing solely on its spiritual content defined elsewhere, we may expand our perspective and account for *all* the available Biblical evidence.

Of course, we cannot simply wave away the literal text of Genesis 1 for convenience, nor can anyone deny that the characters therein are based on reality. The sun, moon, sea creatures, and land animals all literally exist, and believers accept that they were created by God. Our purpose is not to propose otherwise. But we must be very careful, and seek to learn from the text what it has to teach us rather than assuming what that teaching is beforehand.

Certainly, there is always the risk of admitting arbitrary speculation. But, as already noted, simply reading the translated text like a child often doesn't work. Some parts of the Bible are inherently difficult, and arbitrary speculation regarding Genesis 1 abounds, whether we consider its spiritual content or not. In fact, we remain responsible

---

[2] Paul Marston, *Understanding The Biblical Creation Passages,* (Lifesway, 2007), 32. Emphasis mine.
[3] See Appendix II. What Was The Raqia'?

for that spiritual content regardless. So there should be nothing to fear. We should welcome the investigation, and honestly consider if it has any effect on our literal understanding at present.

This means we cannot neglect basic study skills. We look for explicit statements of fact throughout Scripture. We look for Biblical examples, and we look for the instructions by which the Bible encourages us to apply those examples. We do not invent new things for novelty sake, and we acknowledge the historical background of the ancient audience. And if Genesis 1 was intended to convey a meaning beyond face value, the ancient audience would not be made aware of it simply by reading the text in isolation. So then the modern believer should not presume to do so either.

The following table represents a summary of this work as a whole. It provides the reader with a series of statements which, in turn, will be examined and established. The goal is to ensure that our understanding of Genesis 1 does not unintentionally violate the constraints established by the whole of Scripture. Then, and only then, will we have confidence that our literal understanding is viable. In the words of Paul, 'Test everything; hold fast what is good.'[4]

MYSTERY	Genesis 1 presents a hidden, spiritual mystery.
SONG	Genesis 1 conveys a nonliteral sense.
PARABLES	Genesis 1 is associated with parables.
SABBATH	Genesis 1 portrays a sequence of days.
SYMBOLS	Genesis 1 is explained using interchangeable characters.
ALLEGORY	Genesis 1 is a model for the allegory genre in the NT.
DILEMMA	Genesis 1 intentionally differs from other creation texts.

Table 1: Seven Principles Of Genesis 1

---

[4] I Thessalonians 5:21

I.   The Mystery Of Creation

Genesis 1 presents a hidden, spiritual mystery, which is God's plan to include all nations in Jewish promises. This was revealed to the ancient audience by prophetic commentary elsewhere in Scripture.

It is true that the ancient Israelites interpreted the timeline of creation events in Genesis 1 at face value, within the context of their own culture. But not surprisingly, a majority of both Christians and Jews throughout history have also viewed the text as a spiritual representation of events, both past and future. [5] So we too might benefit from an analysis of the spiritual aspects of the text, which are an integral part of it.

To be clear, many different interpretations of the symbols in Genesis 1 have been proposed by others throughout the centuries. And these often reduce to the theological equivalent of pin the tail on the donkey. This is not God's way. We should not ignore the Biblical commentary found elsewhere, which God also gave to Israel, for the express purpose of revealing creation symbolism. Otherwise, we have simply engaged in speculation.

The author of Deutero-Isaiah[6] writes with strong emotion to God's people, from a perspective in exile. Their land had been overrun by

---

[5] Creation abounds with spiritual imagery and types. This suggestion is neither new nor unconventional, and has been understood in various forms. For a thorough historical review, see both Appendix I. The Enigma of Creation, as well as Appendix III. 7000 Years Of Creation?

[6] There is compelling evidence to indicate that Isaiah himself did not actually write the entire book that bears his name. Nevertheless, portions of the traditionally disputed chapters 40-66 are quoted in the NT, and referred to as the words of Isaiah. There are many examples of this, such as Luke 3:4 and 4:17-19. This does not overrule the modern body of evidence which suggests that chapters 40-66 are a compilation of exilic and post exilic texts. It only proves that the prevailing tradition in the first

Assyrian and Babylonian invaders. All seemed lost. And so, Isaiah insists on behalf of God that the Jewish people would be saved from captivity and restored to their land. But Isaiah also presents to Israel a far more potent and universal message, which was based on the text of Genesis 1. His insightful creation commentary in chapters 40-66 forms a Scriptural foundation upon which we may better understand Genesis 1.

Careful study of Isaiah's text reveals three creation principles alongside two unique creation markers. Although he does occasionally make reference to concepts found in other creation texts, the prophet uses these principles and markers to highlight the text of Genesis 1 in particular for his audience.

The first identifying marker is the insistent repetition of the word בָּרָא (bara'), meaning 'to create', which is found in no other OT creation text except Genesis 1. 'Diety is always either the subject or the implied subject (in passive constructions) of the verb. It can therefore be confidently asserted that the activity is inherently a divine activity and not one that humans can perform or participate in.'[7]

The second identifying marker is the insistent repetition of several different words which, in Isaiah's context, appear to be interchangeable references back to the very beginning of the creation of the universe itself. Of these, the word תִּישָׁר (bere'shiyth) is found in no other OT creation text except Genesis 1.

So then it is important that we learn from Isaiah what he intended to teach Israel about that passage.

---

century was to refer to the entire text as 'Isaiah'. Whether that meant they believed one man wrote the whole thing, or whether that meant they believed the quotation came from a compilation text which went by the name 'Isaiah', is another matter entirely. The author is comfortable referring to the contents of the entire book after the manner of the NT authors, for convenience.

[7] John Walton, *The Lost World of Genesis 1*, (InterVarsity Press, 2009), 38.

			CREATE	BEGINNING	
CREATOR	God alone is the Creator of the universe.	40:12, 21-22, 26-28	2x (bara) ברא	(ro'sh) ראש	
		44:21-24			
		48:12-13, 16		(ro'sh) ראש	
		41:2, 4		(ro'sh) ראש	
		41:14, 20-23	(bara) ברא		
		41:25-27		(ro'sh) ראש	
		44:1-3, 7-8			
PROPHET	God alone has the ability to predict events, from the time of creation.	45:7-8, 11-12	4x (bara) ברא		
		45:17-19	2x (bara) ברא		
		46:9-11		(bere'shiyth) ראשית	(qedem) קדם
		48:3-8	(bara) ברא		
		51:13, 15-16			
		54:7-8, 16-17	2x (bara) ברא		
		55:8-11			
		42:1, 5, 9	3x (bara) ברא		
		42:24 - 43:1, 6-7, 9-10, 15	3x (bara) ברא		
VISIONARY	God alone reveals His future spiritual purpose in creation for all nations.	45:20-22	(bara) ברא		
		57:15-19	(bara) ברא	(qedem) קדם	
		65:1, 13-14, 17-18	3x (bara) ברא		

Table 2: Isaiah's Commentary On Genesis 1

Isaiah 40:12, 21, 22, 26-28

'Who has measured the waters in the hollow of his hand and marked off the heavens with a span, enclosed the dust of the earth in a measure and weighed the mountains in scales
and the hills in a balance? ... **Do you not know? Do you not hear? Has it not been told you from the beginning? Have you not understood from the foundations of the earth?** It is He who sits above the circle of the earth, and its inhabitants are like grasshoppers; who stretches out the heavens like a curtain, and spreads them like a tent to dwell in ... Lift up your eyes on high and see: **who created these**? He who brings out their host by number, calling them all by name, by the greatness of His might, and because He is strong in power not one is missing. **Why do you say, O Jacob, and speak, O Israel, 'My way is hidden from the LORD, and my right is disregarded by my God'? Have you not known? Have you not heard?** The LORD is the everlasting God, the Creator of the ends of the earth. He does not faint or grow weary; his understanding is unsearchable.'

Isaiah equates שׁאר (ro'sh) (beginning) with the 'foundation of the earth'. This indicates that creation is under consideration, and several examples of this creation are cited. This emphasis on 'beginning' continues unabated throughout the remainder of Isaiah.

Isaiah's purpose is to correlate Israelite ignorance with this specific time period. Since Israel as a nation was not physically present to witness the creation events, this rhetoric must be interpreted to convey ignorance, in part, of the *meaning* of the creation events. And the object is not simply to identify this deficiency in understanding. The object is also to bring further clarity. This establishes the function of Isaiah's text as creation commentary, starting with chapter 40.

This also establishes the first principle of Isaiah's creation commentary. Although the concept of God as Creator was well known throughout Israel, Isaiah intends to teach them that the implications of that concept were not well known. Israel was instructed to understand what it means to accept God as the Creator.

Isaiah presents Israel as a nation who claims that 'my way is hidden from the LORD'. In other words, they feel that God does not know or care about them as He should. God's response is clear. His power and ability to preserve Israel is evident 'from the beginning', that is as far back as the time of the 'foundation of the earth'. Obviously, Israel had no concept of this else God would not have to repeatedly ask, 'Have you not known?'

Isaiah 41:2, 4

> 'Who stirred up one from the east whom victory meets at every step? He gives up nations before him, so that he tramples kings underfoot; he makes them like dust with his sword, like driven stubble with his bow. …
> Who has performed and done this, calling the generations from the beginning? I, the LORD, the first, and with the last; I am He.'

Depending on the context, the word דּוֹר (dowr) (generations) can refer to a period of time, age, or class of men either past, present, or future. Here the scope of (dowr) (generations) begins with the timeframe of the (ro'sh) (beginning) and continues up until the point where God may refer to himself as being 'with the last'. In other words, God's specific purpose with the 'one from the east', as well as His general purpose with all the generations of man, is spoken of as if it was already finished.

Obviously, God's spiritual plan was not actually finished in Isaiah's day, nor is it yet finished in our own. However, Isaiah's statement that God 'has performed and done this' is not simply an affirmation of God's foreknowledge. That goes without saying. Rather, Isaiah means to communicate a much deeper principle. Not only did God know, within Himself, the details of His plan for the generations of mankind, but also He אָרָק (qara') (called, proclaimed, cried out) concerning those plans. This loud proclamation by God concerning the future occurred in the (ro'sh) (beginning), and is equivocated specifically with the actions of God in that same (ro'sh) (beginning).

This then is the second principle of Isaiah's commentary on creation. He intends to teach Israel that the creation reveals God's plans for the future.

Isaiah 41:14, 20-23

> 'Fear not, you worm Jacob, you men of Israel! I am the one who helps you, declares the LORD; your Redeemer is the Holy One of Israel. ... that they may see and know, may consider and understand together, that the hand of the LORD has done this, the Holy One of Israel has created it. Set forth your case, says the LORD; bring your proofs, says the King of Jacob. Let them bring them, and tell us what is to happen. Tell us the former things, what they are, that we may consider them, that we may know their outcome; or declare to us the things to come. Tell us what is to come hereafter, that we may know that you are gods; do good, or do harm, that we may be dismayed and terrified.'

After declaring 'Fear not...I am the one who helps you', God turns the table on Israel and challenges them to duplicate a truly amazing feat. He dares them to predict things before they occur, as early as the time 'from the beginning'. Obviously Israel cannot answer God's challenge, but the real question is why God would challenge them to such an impossible task in the first place. God doesn't really expect Israel to be able to comply. On the contrary, He merely expects them to realize that He has already completed said feat. God intends to prove His authority and power through His fulfilled predictions.

But Israel was not yet aware of this principle. If they were, they would have no reason to fear. God had 'declared from the beginning' His promise to 'help' Israel. Isaiah literally says that the 'Holy One of Israel has (bara') (created) it', in reference to the aforementioned Divine 'help'.

The word (ro'sh) (beginning) is used here as before, and now a new word is added for effect. The word is רִאשׁוֹן (ri'shown), translated 'former things', and meaning 'first, primary, former, chief'. Of course, the 'former things' are much more than just arbitrary things which happened in the past. They are critical events in Israel's history, which God had planned beforehand.

Isaiah 41:25-27

> 'I stirred up one from the north, and he has come, from the rising of the sun, and he shall call upon my name; he shall trample on rulers as on mortar, as the potter treads clay. Who declared it from the beginning, that we might know, and beforehand, that we might say, 'He is right'? There was none who declared it, none who proclaimed, none who heard your words. I was the first to say to Zion, 'Behold, here they are!' and I give to Jerusalem a herald of good news.'

This prophecy also specifically relates to a 'declaration from the (ro'sh) (beginning)'. The greater context remains the promised 'help' for Israel, discussed above, and so we see that the 'one from the north...from the rising of the sun' is in fact the 'help' for Israel. He was both 'declared' and (bara') (created), conceptually. God contrasts His ability to predict the events ahead of time with the fact that Israel could not do the same. His predictions 'from the beginning' were put in place so that we might conclude that 'He is right'. But 'no one heard your words,' says the prophet!

Isaiah 42:1, 5, 9

> 'Behold my servant, whom I uphold, my chosen, in whom my soul delights; I have put my Spirit upon him; he will bring forth justice to the nations. ... Thus says God, the LORD, who created the heavens and stretched them out, who spread out the earth and what comes from it, who gives breath to the people on it and spirit to those who walk in it: ... Behold, the former things have come to pass, and new things I now declare; before they spring forth I tell you of them.'

Now then, Isaiah expands his commentary on creation. He distinguishes between God's ability to predict 'former' things, and God's ability to predict 'new' things. The word for 'former' is, as before, (ri'shown) (first, primary, former, chief). Considering the overt references to creation in verse 5, as well as the consistent theme of creation up to this point, it is quite reasonable to presume that the focus remains unchanged. What's more, Isaiah says that these 'former' things are 'come to pass'. That is to say that the 'former' events are fulfilled predictions. To remove all doubt on this matter, Isaiah reiterates that God tells things 'before they spring forth'.

This establishes the third principle of Isaiah's creation commentary. Just as God has predicted 'former things', from the time that He 'created the heavens and...spread out the earth', so too does God predict 'justice to the nations' as a 'new thing'. This is revolutionary teaching, which Israel in general did not comprehend. As Creator of all nations, God is manifestly able to save those of any nationality, even those who were not born Jewish. But we cannot lose sight of the source of this wonderful principle, which allows so many of us to be part of the hope and promises of God. The very source of this theological truth is the revelation of creation itself. Isaiah explicitly tells Israel that God has revealed these things from the 'beginning'. And, more specifically, he focuses on the text of Genesis 1 to make his case.

Isaiah 42:24 - 43:1, 6-7, 9-10, 15

> 'Who gave up Jacob to the looter, and Israel to the plunderers? Was it not the LORD, against whom we have sinned, in whose ways they would not walk, and whose law they would not obey? So he poured on him the heat of his anger and the might of battle; it set him on fire all around, but he did not understand; it burned him up, but he did not take it to heart. But now thus says the LORD, he who created you, O Jacob, he who formed you, O Israel: 'Fear not, for I have redeemed you; I have called you by name, you are mine. ... I will say to the north, Give up, and to the south, Do not withhold; bring my sons from afar and my daughters from the end of the earth, everyone who is called by my name, whom I created for my glory, whom I formed and made....All the nations gather together, and the peoples assemble. Who among them can declare this, and show us the former things? Let them bring their witnesses to prove them right, and let them hear and say, It is true. 'You are my witnesses,' declares the LORD, 'and my servant whom I have chosen, that you may know and believe me and understand that I am he. Before me no god was formed, nor shall there be any after me. ... I am the LORD, your Holy One, the Creator of Israel, your King.'

Isaiah points out a great irony here. Not only did Israel not understand their 'help', as predicted 'from the beginning', so too they did not understand it was God Himself who was punishing them for their transgressions. Notwithstanding this fact, God promises that Israel will be redeemed. As a result of God's promised protection and salvation, He again demands to know if *any* of 'all the nations' can 'declare this and show us (ri'shown) (former) things.' This they cannot do, and so God concludes that Israel herself constitutes 'my witnesses'. The people themselves, as a nation, are verifiable evidence that God has 'declared and shown (ri'shown) former things'.

But to whom is Israel a witness? To 'all the nations', of course! This is the obvious result of God's logic, as described by the prophet. The creation of all humanity is cited as evidence, and in this regard Isaiah specifically echoes Genesis 1. He refers to 'everyone who is called by my name, whom I created for my glory, whom I formed and made.' This reflects the equality and dominion conferred to humanity in Genesis 1. It also reflects the image and likeness of God, which is conferred to humanity in Genesis 1. God even states that He (bara') (created) and רֲצָי yatsar (formed) Israel. It is abundantly clear, therefore, that the spiritual focus of creation hinges upon God's plans for and protection of Israel, which necessarily includes non-Jewish people.

Isaiah 44: 1-3, 7, 8

> 'But now hear, O Jacob my servant, Israel whom I have chosen! Thus says the LORD **who made you, who formed you from the womb and will help you**: Fear not, O Jacob my servant, Jeshurun whom I have chosen. For I will pour water on the thirsty land, and streams on the dry ground; I will pour my Spirit upon your offspring, and my blessing on your descendants. ... Who is like me? Let him proclaim it. **Let him declare and set it before me, since I appointed an ancient people. Let them declare what is to come, and what will happen.** Fear not, nor be afraid; **have I not told you from of old and declared it?** And you are my witnesses! Is there a God besides me? There is no Rock; I know not any.'

God refers to Israel, this time as the 'ancient people'. The word for 'ancient' is (owlam), which at the very least refers to 'a very long time ago'. However, coupling this phrase with the immediate context shows us that God 'appointed the ancient people' all the way back when He (yatsar) (formed) Israel.

Perhaps we might assume that this is only referring back to the time period of the Exodus, or perhaps back to the covenants made with Abraham. And that would be true, in a technical sense. But we cannot upset the continuity of Isaiah's creation theme. The sheer volume of references to the creation by Isaiah insist that God formulated His plan for His people ahead of time. The text of Genesis 1 reveals spiritual principles from that time, so to speak. From a theological, or spiritual, perspective, it makes no difference that the text was not actually written down from the moment of creation. Nor does it matter that God did not formally initiate the nation of Israel until the time of Abraham. That is not the point that Isaiah intends to communicate.

So then God follows up the 'appointment of the ancient people' with the affirmation '*I told you from that time*!' What did God tell Israel, and when did He tell them? He told them 'the things that are coming, and shall come', from the time when He (yatsar) (formed) Israel. That is creation, from God's perspective. See also Isaiah 44:21-24. 'Ye are my witnesses' God declares, concerning the unwitting and undeserving people.

Isaiah 44:21-24

> 'Remember these things, O Jacob, and Israel, for you are my servant; **I formed you**; you are my servant; O Israel, you will not be forgotten by me. I have blotted out your transgressions like a cloud and your sins like mist; return to me, for I have redeemed you. **Sing, O heavens, for the LORD has done it; shout, O depths of the earth**; break forth into singing, O mountains, O forest, and every tree in it! For the LORD has redeemed Jacob, and will be glorified in Israel. Thus says the LORD, your Redeemer, **who formed you from the womb**: 'I am the LORD, who made all things, **who alone stretched out the heavens, who spread out the earth by myself**.' '

God directly compares here the (yatsar) (forming) of Israel to the creation of all other things, such as the heavens, the earth, mountains, trees, etc. This is further evidence to indicate that when God speaks prophetically of (yatsar) (forming) Israel, He does not limit Himself to the time of Abraham or the Exodus. The very creation, that is Genesis 1, is ultimately in view. Israel's origin is also symbolized as a child's formation in the womb, and God commands all the other created things to sing and shout because 'the LORD hath...glorified Himself in Israel.' Thus, the prophet declares that God's role as Creator of things is inseparable from His role as Creator of Israel. This makes sense. Isaiah's commentary on creation intends to provide evidence by which God may justify Himself to Israel.

Isaiah 45:7-8, 11, 12

> '**I form light and create darkness**, I make well-being and create calamity, I am the LORD, who does all these things. Shower, O heavens, from above, and let the clouds rain down righteousness; let the earth open, that salvation and righteousness may bear fruit; let the earth cause them both to sprout; **I the LORD have created it.** ... Thus says the LORD, the Holy One of Israel, and **the one who formed him**: **Ask me of things to come; will you command me concerning my children and the work of my hands**? I made the earth and created man on it; it was my hands that stretched out the heavens, and I commanded all their host.'

Yet again, God deliberately recalls Genesis 1, with references to the 'creation of light and darkness' and again 'the Lord has (bara') (created) 'salvation and righteousness'. God also demands that his audience seek a sign from Him. 'Ask me of things to come'. And just what exactly are those 'things to come'? They are 'concerning my sons, and concerning the work of my hands... I have made the earth.' So then the sign is creation, and that same creation does in fact represent future events, or 'things to come'. God equates His people Israel with the creation, i.e. 'my sons'.

Isaiah 45:17-19

> '**But Israel is saved by the LORD with everlasting salvation**; you shall not be put to shame or confounded to all eternity. For thus says the LORD, **who created the heavens (He is God!), who formed the earth and**

made it (He established it; He did not create it empty,
He formed it to be inhabited!): I am the LORD, and
there is no other. **I did not speak in secret, in a land of
darkness**; I did not say to the offspring of Jacob, Seek
me in vain. I the LORD speak the truth; I declare what is
right.'

Isaiah refuses to allow the attentive reader to stray from the events
of Genesis 1. God's ability to create the heavens and the earth is
rendered useless, if said creation were not given a specific purpose.
Isaiah says the purpose of the creation is 'to be inhabited'. By
virtue of the fact that Isaiah is speaking to Israel, he infers that the
creation is to be inhabited specifically by Israel. This purpose
should have been understood from the text of Genesis 1, or 'from
the beginning'.

Verse 19 is a particularly useful example with which to illustrate
this point. God said 'I did not speak in secret'. 'I did not say to the
offspring of Jacob, Seek me in vain'. That is to say that the
revelation of creation should have provided evidence to Israel of
God's care for them. He did not expect them to follow Him for no
reason. But the significance of this concept, derived from creation,
would seem to have been missed. So then we have confirmation
that Isaiah's commentary on creation was a necessary supplement.
Israel's inability to grasp God's purpose with creation elicited God's
decision to speak once more. See also 46:9-11 and 48:3-8, 16
below.

Isaiah 45:20-22

'Assemble yourselves and come; draw near together, **you
survivors of the nations!** They have no knowledge who
carry about their wooden idols, and keep on praying to a
god that cannot save. Declare and present your case; let
them take counsel together! **Who told this long ago?
Who declared it of old? Was it not I, the LORD**? And
there is no other god besides me, a righteous God and a
Savior; there is none besides me. **Turn to me and be
saved, all the ends of the earth!** For I am God, and
there is no other.'

The word here for 'long ago' is קֶדֶם (qedem) (ancient time). God
has declared from (qedem) (ancient time) that 'the nations' are

included in His plan for Israel's salvation. He tells them all 'be ye saved, all the ends of the earth!' Taken by itself, (qedem) (ancient time) does not require a reference all the way back to the creation, but the author asserts once more that the obvious repetition by Isaiah up to this point leaves us with no other choice. It appears that Isaiah himself would agree with this assertion, based on his own usage of (qedem) in the next passage below.

Isaiah 46:9-11

> 'Remember the former things of old; for I am God, and there is no other; I am God, and there is none like me, declaring the end from the beginning and from ancient times things not yet done, saying, 'My counsel shall stand, and I will accomplish all my purpose', calling a bird of prey from the east, the man of my counsel from a far country. I have spoken, and I will bring it to pass; I have purposed, and I will do it.'

In this quote, Isaiah explicitly connects (ri'shown) (first, primary, former, chief) with (bere'shiyth) (first, beginning) and (qedem) (ancient time). This is a critical point which illustrates the continuity of Isaiah's prophetic references to the creation, rather than the time period of the Exodus, or the time period of the covenants made with Abraham, or any other time period of history which might otherwise be inserted here. When did God declare 'the end'? From 'the beginning'!

Indeed, the very word (bere'shiyth) isolates Genesis 1 as the particular text in view. Recall that there is no other creation text in the Bible which identifies itself in this manner. And there can be no question that God's purpose 'in the (bere'shiyth) (first, beginning)' was to 'speak' first, and then 'bring it pass'; to 'purpose' it, and then 'do it'. The creative process in Genesis 1 follows this format with great precision. It constitutes the spoken word of God, predicting future events before they happened, and God intends to make Israel aware of this through Isaiah's creation commentary. This explains Isaiah's persistent Bible echo of the 'beginning' theme.

Keep in mind, however, both what God did and did not intend to predict 'from the beginning'. Being in exile, the writer of Isaiah admits that God has already punished Israel with captivity in

Babylon, e.g. 42:24-25. Israel should now be looking for the restoration of Jerusalem and the temple, by the authority of Cyrus the Mede, e.g. 44:26-28, 46:11. But specific details like these cannot possibly be inferred from the creation text of Genesis 1 alone. So as we have said, this is creation commentary. This information is both necessary and supplemental.

Isaiah 48:3-8

> 'The former things I declared of old; they went out from my mouth, and I announced them; then suddenly I did them, and they came to pass. Because I know that you are obstinate, and your neck is an iron sinew and your forehead brass, I declared them to you from of old, before they came to pass I announced them to you, lest you should say, 'My idol did them, my carved image and my metal image commanded them. You have heard; now see all this; and will you not declare it? From this time forth I announce to you new things, hidden things that you have not known. They are created now, not long ago; before today you have never heard of them, lest you should say, 'Behold, I knew them. You have never heard, you have never known, from of old your ear has not been opened. For I knew that you would surely deal treacherously, and that from before birth you were called a rebel.'

This time the (ri'shown) (first, primary, former, chief) things are equated with אז ('az) (sometime in the past). Isaiah's previously cited connections between (ri'shown), (bere'shiyth), and (qedem) cannot be disregarded. He insists on maintaining this creation theme, using repetitive language for dramatic effect.

And God has given a specific reason for 'declaring and showing things from the beginning'. He wished to preempt Israel's fascination with false gods, and lay claim to His own accomplishments before they occurred. Just as in 42:1, 5, 9, Isaiah refers here to 'new' predictions, in contrast with (ri'shown) (former) predictions. So then we acknowledge that these 'new' predictions are spoken of as being (bara') (created) now, in contrast with the creation 'long ago'. Isaiah's use of the word (bara') in this manner verifies the inspired metonymy which he continues to draw from Genesis 1. Creation and prophecy are inexorably linked.

But God also explains His purpose with Isaiah's creation commentary. He certainly could have included additional information in the original text of Genesis 1, but He did not. 'From this time forth I announce to you new things...before today you have never heard of them, lest you should say, 'Behold, I knew them'.' This arises from the fact that God declares Israel to be 'a rebel from the womb'. It is neither possible to physically rebel before one is born, nor can a specific transgression be literally applied to an entire nation prior to its existence. And so this statement from God can only be taken to mean what the greater context has already communicated to us. God has predicted the rebellion of Israel 'before it came to pass', when He (bara') (created) and (yatsar) (formed) Israel 'in the beginning'.

The decision to separate the spiritual commentary of Genesis 1 from its source text is very instructive. It was a decision made by God, because He knew the sinful tendencies of His people. It is a model for exposition which Christ himself would later follow, in the NT.

Isaiah 48:12-13, 16

> 'Listen to me, O Jacob, and Israel, whom I called! I am he; I am the first, and I am the last. My hand laid the foundation of the earth, and my right hand spread out the heavens; when I call to them, they stand forth together. ... Draw near to me, hear this: from the beginning I have not spoken in secret, from the time it came to be I have been there. And now the Lord GOD has sent me, and his Spirit.'

Now, God follows His thesis to its logical conclusion. He commands Israel to listen and draw near to Him, on the premise that they have acknowledged Him as Creator. While this premise appears mildly significant, in truth it is much more than that. God's claim to the physical creation alone cannot be *empirically* verified by anyone, in any time period. Therefore, God's fulfilled predictions from within the creation text are the substantive proof He has provided to justify Himself in the eyes of Israel, upon which He demands their allegiance.

God also reminds Israel that He has not 'spoken in secret' from the (ro'sh) (beginning), just as in 45:19. This reiterates the necessity of Divine commentary in the text of Isaiah concerning creation. If Israel had grasped the necessary spiritual and prophetic elements from the revelation of Genesis 1 alone, God would not have to repeatedly clarify Himself through Isaiah in the way that He does.

Isaiah 51:9, 13, 15-16

> '..and **have forgotten the LORD, your Maker, who stretched out the heavens and laid the foundations of the earth, and you fear continually all the day** because of the wrath of the oppressor, when he sets himself to destroy? And where is the wrath of the oppressor? ... I am the LORD your God, who stirs up the sea so that its waves roar— the LORD of hosts is his name. And I have put my words in your mouth and covered you in the shadow of my hand, **establishing the heavens and laying the foundations of the earth, and saying to Zion, 'You are my people.'**

Because Israel 'forgot God', and did not understand the implications of God as Creator, they 'feared continually'. They did not perceive God's predictions and intent to 'help' them. Nonetheless, God through Isaiah summarizes His grand treatise on the creation by equating the call of 'my people, Zion' with the 'planting of the heavens' and the 'laying of the foundation of the earth.' As far as God is concerned, they are all one and the same event. His plans were indeed declared and shown 'from the beginning'.

Isaiah 54:7-8, 16-17

> 'For a brief moment I deserted you, but with great
> compassion I will gather you. In overflowing anger for
> a moment I hid my face from you, but with everlasting
> love I will have compassion on you, says the LORD,
> your Redeemer. ... Behold, I have created the smith
> who blows the fire of coals and produces a weapon for
> its purpose. I have also created the ravager to
> destroy; no weapon that is fashioned against you shall
> succeed, and you shall refute every tongue that rises
> against you in judgment. This is the heritage of the
> servants of the LORD and their vindication from me,
> declares the LORD.'

Once more the writer speaks from a position of exile, accepting the
'brief moment' of desertion by God and looking forward in
anticipation to the 'vindication' of Israel. This 'anger', though, is
part of God's intentional process with His people. And so we see
again that God has (bara') (created) both the agents and the
weaponry of this punishment, using the creation language of
Genesis 1.

Isaiah 55:8-11

> 'For my thoughts are not your thoughts, neither are
> your ways my ways, declares the LORD. For as the
> heavens are higher than the earth, so are my ways
> higher than your ways and my thoughts than your
> thoughts. For as the rain and the snow come down from
> heaven and do not return there but water the earth,
> making it bring forth and sprout, giving seed to the sower
> and bread to the eater, so shall my word be that goes
> out from my mouth; it shall not return to me empty,
> but it shall accomplish that which I purpose, and shall
> succeed in the thing for which I sent it.'

God explicitly compares His 'thoughts' and 'ways' with the features
and functions of the physical creation. He also compares the
specific, creative technique utilized in Genesis 1, that being 'my
word that goes out from my mouth', as representative of His intent
to accomplish His purposes. Now that we have established a

significant precedent of emphasis on creation throughout Isaiah, this reference takes on a much deeper meaning for the faithful in Israel.

Isaiah 57:15-19

> 'For thus says the One who is high and lifted up,
> who inhabits eternity, whose name is Holy:
> '**I dwell in the high and holy place,**
> **and also with him who is of a contrite and lowly**
> **spirit**,
> to revive the spirit of the lowly, and to revive the heart of
> the contrite. **For I will not contend forever, nor will I**
> **always be angry**; for the spirit would grow faint before
> me, **and the breath of life that I made. Because of the**
> **iniquity of his unjust gain I was angry, I struck him**; I
> hid my face and was angry, but he went on backsliding
> in the way of his own heart. I have seen his ways, **but I**
> **will heal him; I will lead him and restore comfort to**
> **him and his mourners, creating the fruit of the lips.**
> **Peace, peace, to the far and to the near,**' says the
> LORD, 'and I will heal him.'

God acknowledges the certain end of His people, if He were not to turn again from their punishment. 'I struck him', God says, 'but I will heal him.' The very creation would otherwise be of no use, and the 'breath of life' would 'grow faint'. So God intends to (bara') (create) the 'fruit of the lips' which is 'peace'. But this 'peace' extends both to those who are 'near' as well as those who are 'far'. This requires that other nations be included, as Isaiah has already told us.

And this is precisely the circumstance we find at the end of Genesis 1. The work of creation is complete, and there is no possibility of conflict. The male and female have dominion over all, and God rests. Isaiah insists that his audience recognize these theological principles, which the text of Genesis 1 reflects.

Isaiah 65:1, 13-14, 17-18

> 'I was ready to be sought **by those who did not ask for**
> **me**;
> I was ready to be found **by those who did not seek me. I**
> said, 'Here I am, here I am,' **to a nation that was not**

called by my name. I spread out my hands all the day to a rebellious people,
who walk in a way that is not good, following their own devices… Therefore thus says the Lord GOD: 'Behold, **my servants shall eat, but you shall be hungry**; behold, **my servants shall drink, but you shall be thirsty**; behold, **my servants shall rejoice, but you shall be put to shame**; behold, my servants shall sing for gladness of heart, but you shall cry out for pain of heart and shall wail for breaking of spirit. … For behold, **I create new heavens and a new earth**, and the former things shall not be remembered or come into mind. **But be glad and rejoice forever in that which I create**. For behold, I create Jerusalem to be a joy, and her people to be a gladness.'

In a grand climax, the creation commentary of Isaiah once more reveals that other nations would be involved in God's wonderful salvation. God does not choose, simply on the basis of physical genealogy, but rather on the basis that we 'walk in a way that is good' and respond to Him in sincerity. Gentiles who were 'not called by my name' would nevertheless 'eat', 'drink', and 'rejoice' in the 'new heavens and earth' which God (bara') (creates). On the other hand, Jews who were called by God's name would 'cry out for pain' and 'wail for breaking of spirit'. And this new heavens and earth is necessarily reflected in the text of Genesis 1. That text has been the specific focus of the prophet for twenty six chapters.

It should come as no surprise therefore to find that Isaiah's creation commentary also takes center stage in the NT.

The apostle Paul confirms the words of Isaiah where he states, 'But we impart **a secret and hidden wisdom** of God, **which God decreed before the ages for our glory**.'[8] Just as in the case of Isaiah 41:4, which states God אָרָק (qara') (called, proclaimed, cried out) concerning his planned actions, Paul also tells us that God 'decreed' His 'secret wisdom' 'before the ages'. It is not reasonable for Paul to make this claim, if we have no way to verify it. So then what had been hidden by the physical creation itself is made known through God's revelation of that physical creation in a written text. The teaching of Genesis 1 should hold the key to this 'secret', as

---

[8] I Corinthians 2:7

Isaiah indicates. It is the OT text which most closely corresponds to the time period described.

Paul informs us that, 'Now to him who is able to strengthen you according to my gospel and the preaching of Jesus Christ, according to the **revelation of the mystery that was kept secret for long ages but has now been disclosed and through the prophetic writings** has been made known to all nations, according to the command of the eternal God, to bring about the obedience of faith.'[9] Paul indicates that the original revelation of this 'mystery' was *not* the NT texts, but rather the OT prophets. This confirms the interpretations above, and requires that God's 'secret decree' be contained within a written, preserved text. The OT texts are therefore to be interpreted as such, and confirmed in light of new revelation.

Of further importance is the detail here which indicates that the 'secret' was 'kept' 'for long ages'. The Greek χρόνος (chronos) (time) αἰώνιος (aiōnios) (ages), here translated 'long ages', is elsewhere translated by the ESV more definitively as 'before the ages began'.[10] This makes sense, and agrees directly with numerous other translations of the quote here from Romans 16. So the 'secret' from 'before the ages began' does stem from Genesis 1, being the foundation text which contains the key to said 'mystery'. This also verifies our previous findings in Isaiah 45:19 and 48:16, where God declared 'I have not spoken in secret from the beginning'.

Paul again emphasizes this most important point so that that there can be no mistake. 'When you read this, you can perceive my insight into **the mystery of Christ, which was not made known to the sons of men in other generations as it has now been revealed to his holy apostles and prophets by the Spirit**..... and to bring to light for everyone what is **the plan of the mystery hidden for ages in God who created all things.**'[11] Paul, following the lead of Isaiah, is careful to connect the theme of creation to the 'mystery of Christ' 'hidden for ages'. This is precisely what we know Isaiah has already told us. The hidden mystery revealed in Genesis 1 enhances

---

[9] Romans 16:25-26
[10] II Timothy 1:9; Titus 1:2
[11] Ephesians 3:4-6, 9

the glory of the great God of the Ages, who delights in representing things 'before they come to pass'.

Indeed, the honor falls to Paul to explicitly confirm and summarize this mystery for the NT audience. 'When you read this, you can perceive my insight into the mystery of Christ … **This mystery is that the Gentiles are fellow heirs, members of the same body, and partakers of the promise in Christ Jesus through the gospel.**'[12]

Paul's declaration is utterly appropriate, for it was he who was 'the minister of Jesus Christ to the Gentiles'[13], 'according to the stewardship of God that was given'[14] to him. But even more than that, the Gentiles were never an afterthought. Their inclusion in God's plot was in fact predicted 'from the beginning'. Paul cites two different passages from Isaiah's creation commentary in Romans 15 alone, to teach this principle.[15] His own understanding of the prophet's words is self-evident. But to this wonderful revelation the Jews were blinded.[16] Not by virtue of the fact that God had not revealed it to them, but simply because they refused to accept it.

Once more, to the church at Colosse, Paul states his purpose was 'to make the word of God fully known, **the mystery hidden for ages and generations** but now revealed to His saints. To them God chose to make known **how great among the Gentiles are the riches of the glory of this mystery**, which is Christ in you, the hope of glory.'[17] So then there can be no reasonable doubt. 'The mystery hidden for ages' can be none other than the spiritual predictions of God found in the timeline of events in Genesis 1. It represents God's future purpose for all nations as part of His creation.

Perhaps the reader expected that this mysterious secret would have been something much more complicated. Or perhaps the reader

---

[12] Ibid
[13] Romans 15:16
[14] Colossians 1:25
[15] Isaiah 11:10; 52:15
[16] John 12:39-40; II Corinthians 3:13-16; etc.
[17] Colossians 1:25-27

may have already known about some of the concepts behind this mystery. Regardless, the author insists that the reader take careful note. Our knowledge of this mystery, after the fact, does nothing to affect its status as a Biblically defined 'mystery'. The term itself remains the preferred description of the principle at hand.

And the reason for this is simple. Genesis 1 is God's mystery, and not our own. Genesis 1 represents God's theological covenant timeline, and not our own. So our spiritual understanding of it must conform to the guidelines established by Scripture, i.e. the constraints of Isaiah's creation commentary. We have no choice but to place the origin of this mysterious covenant 'in the beginning', so to speak, right where it always was.

II.   The Song Of Creation

Genesis 1 conveys a nonliteral sense.   It is a
theatrical witness, both to the collapse of God's old
covenant with Israel, as well as to the future success
of God's new covenant with all nations.

The Song of Moses, as recorded in Deut. 32, was embedded into the
minds of the people at a very early stage in Israel's history. And it
clearly establishes the spiritual function of creation in a non-literal
sense. Eventually, the Song of Moses would form the basis of
Deutero-Isaiah's commentary on Genesis 1. So then, we might also
refer to the Song of Moses as the Song of Creation.

God declares, 'Now therefore write this Song and teach it to the
people of Israel. Put it in their mouths, that this Song may be a
witness for me against the people of Israel. ... And when many evils
and troubles have come upon them, this Song shall confront them as
a witness (for it will live unforgotten in the mouths of their
offspring).'[18]

Deuteronomy 31:28, 30; 32:1, 4, 15-16, 43

> 'Assemble to me all the elders of your tribes and your
> officers, that I may speak these words in their ears and
> **call heaven and earth to witness against them.** ...
> Then Moses spoke the words of this song until they were
> finished, in the ears of all the assembly of Israel: **Give
> ear, O heavens, and I will speak, and let the earth
> hear** the words of my mouth. ...
> **The Rock**, his work is perfect, for all his ways are
> justice.
> A God of faithfulness and without iniquity, just and
> upright is He ... But **Jeshurun grew fat**, and kicked;
> you grew fat, stout, and sleek; then he forsook God who

---

[18] Deut. 31:19, 21

> made him and **scoffed at the Rock** of his salvation. They
> stirred him to jealousy with strange gods; with
> abominations they provoked him to anger. ... **Rejoice
> with him, O heavens**; bow down to him, all gods, for he
> avenges the blood of his children and takes vengeance on
> his adversaries. He repays those who hate him and
> cleanses his people's land.'

The express purpose of the Song was to communicate to Israel
important predictions of future events, and confirm God's covenant
with them. The Song predicts Israel's rebellion against God after
the death of Moses[19], as well as their ultimate salvation from
destruction by God's mercy.[20]

It is striking to note that Moses calls the very creation itself, namely
'the heaven and the earth', to give attention to the evidence
presented against Israel. It is even more striking, when we realize
that Moses actually speaks to the heaven and earth throughout the
Song, not as inanimate physical objects, but rather as conscious
participants in his three way address. He acts as a mediator between
the people of Israel, and 'the heaven and the earth', speaking the
words of God. The use of the third person pronoun 'they', with
reference to Israel, in both the opening and closing lines of the Song
show this. God intends to represent 'the heaven and the earth' as
the aggregate witness against Israel for their future rebellion.

Therefore, the Song of Moses constitutes God's predictive
declaration via Moses *to* 'the heaven and the earth' *about* what
Israel will do. The opening statement of the Song is much more
important than might be supposed. 'Give ear, O heavens, and I will
speak, and let the earth hear the words of my mouth!' The primary
recipients of the Song's message are 'the heaven and the earth'.
Israel is actually a third party in this case; merely an uninformed and
mystified audience.

This is not mere grammatical oddity.[21] The seamless transitions
between the words spoken to 'the heaven and the earth', and the

---

[19] Deut. 31:20-21
[20] Deut. 32:43
[21] 'Huffmon, 'Covenant Lawsuit,' 292–93, explains that in ancient Near
Eastern treaties, natural elements were summoned as witnesses not because

words spoken to Israel, effectively places Moses in a courtroom before a jury and the accused.

THE SONG	OF CREATION
Duet 31:28 - 32:43	Isaiah 1; 44; 49
Give ear, O heavens, and I will **speak**, and **let the earth hear** the words of my mouth - Deut 32:1	**Hear, O heavens**, and **give ear, O earth**; for the LORD **has spoken** - Isaiah 1:2
	Listen to me, O coastlands, and give attention, **you peoples from afar** - Isaiah 49:1
The Rock, his work is perfect, for all his ways are justice - Deut 32:4	Is there a God besides me? **There is no Rock**; I know not any - Isaiah 44:8
They have **dealt corruptly** with him; they are **no longer his children** - Deut 32:5	Ah, sinful nation, a people laden with iniquity, offspring of evildoers, **children who deal corruptly** - Isaiah 1:4
because they are **blemished**; they are a crooked and twisted generation - Duet 32:5	From the sole of the foot even to the head, there is no soundness in it, but **bruises and sores and raw wounds** - Isaiah 1:6

they belonged to the divine assembly but 'because the curses and blessings—part of the covenant—involved these natural phenomena.' However, the meaning that the natural elements played as witnesses for Israel is not clear. It may follow the meaning of the ancient Near Eastern treaties. Huffmon suggests 'that heaven and earth served as judges, for Yahweh as the plaintiff and Israel the accursed. Heaven and earth as judges may be a literary fiction, but it would be more appropriate if the judge could serve as the executor of the sentence in actual court practice (as is suggested by Deuteronomy 25:1–3), **since the natural world served to carry out the curses and blessings**'' Emphasis mine. See Rene Lopez, 'Israelite Covenants in the Light of Ancient Near Eastern Covenants', *CTS Journal*, 10 (Spring 2004), 83-84. <http://chafer.nextmeta.com/files/v10n1_5lopez_covenants2israelite_cove nants.pdf>

But **Jeshurun** grew fat, and kicked;... You were unmindful of **the Rock** that bore you, and **you forgot the God who gave you birth** - Deut 32:15, 18	Thus says the LORD who made you, **who formed you from the womb** and will help you: Fear not, O Jacob my servant, **Jeshurun** whom I have chosen - Isaiah 44:2
	The LORD called me **from the womb**, from the body of his mother he named my name. - Isaiah 49:1
For they are a nation **void of counsel**, and there is **no understanding** in them - Deut 32:28	The ox knows its owner, and the donkey its master's crib, but Israel **does not know**, my people **do not understand** - Isaiah 1:3
For their vine comes from the **vine of Sodom** and from the **fields of Gomorrah** - Deut 32:32	Hear the word of the LORD, you rulers of **Sodom**! Give ear to the teaching of our God, you people of **Gomorrah** - Isaiah 1:10
Vengeance is mine, and recompense, for the time when their foot shall slip - Deut 32:35	Ah, I will get relief from my enemies and **avenge myself on my foes** - Isaiah 1:24

Rejoice with him, O heavens; bow down to him, all gods, for he **avenges the blood of his children**, and takes vengeance on his adversaries. - Deut 32:43	**Return to me**, for I have redeemed you. **Sing, O heavens**, for the LORD has done it; shout, O depths of the earth - Isaiah 44:22-23
	Sing for joy, O heavens, and exult, O earth … For the LORD has comforted his people and **will have compassion on his afflicted**. - Isaiah 49:13

Table 3: The Song Of Creation

Centuries later, both Isaiah and Deutero-Isaiah deliberately mimic the format of the Song of Moses. They recall how Israel had fulfilled the predictions of God through Moses by way of their rebellion. As seen from the table above, the Song of Moses is referenced on numerous occasions to make the point clear. This puts in perspective Isaiah's proclamation of Israelite ignorance concerning God's teaching 'from the beginning'. Israel of course understood, in a technical sense, both the concept of God as Creator as well as the words of the Song of Moses. But as stated before, they neither realized the implications of those words nor the meaning of 'the heaven and earth' as a functional witness against them. Therefore, Isaiah calls 'the heaven and earth' to witness against Israel again and again in his commentary on Genesis 1. The correlation between the Song of Moses and the words of Isaiah verifies that both texts share the same overall purpose.

'There are additional features in the context which argue for a dependency between these two texts in the use of 'Rock' as an appellation of the Lord. In Deut. 32:5 Jeshurun appears as a name for Israel. This name appears again in this portion of Isaiah's prophecy. In fact, **this is the only occurrence of this name outside of the Song and Blessing of Moses** (Deuteronomy 32 and 33). Thus, the only time the Lord is referred to as "Rock" and Israel is referred to as Jeshurun in the same context is the Song of Moses and one small passage of II Isaiah. However, the connections do not end there. In both passages the name "Eloah" is used for God (Deut. 32:15; Isa. 44:8).

> The fact that this is the only time that that specific name is used in Isaiah makes this connection even more significant, since it is obviously not a common expression for the author(s). However, the association is still greater in that in both passages the name Eloah is used in parallelism with "Rock".
>
> Based on the uniqueness of the term Jeshurun, the peculiar usage of the name Eloah, all in association with the reference to the Lord as the "Rock", and within a context which makes the same theological point (the incomparability of Yahweh) in the same situation (Israel's failure), **it appears that there is a direct and conscious dependency between Isaiah 44 and Deuteronomy 32.**'[22]

In Isaiah 49, we find further evidence for this conclusion. Notice the similarities between the words of Isaiah and the words of the Song of Moses. 'Listen to me, O coastlands, and give attention, you peoples from afar.' Isaiah begins by speaking to inanimate objects of creation, just as Moses does, and demands their attention. But then, he equates that creation with 'peoples from afar' and 'nations'. Isaiah even matches Moses in his conclusion. 'Sing for joy, O heavens, and exult, O earth; break forth, O mountains, into singing.' This is far from mere coincidence.

The reader should now consider why God, through Moses and Isaiah, repeatedly speaks to 'the heaven and the earth'? How can those elements be a witness against Israel, and evidence of future predictions? It is precisely because the Song of Moses was **audibly** rehearsed by Israel in the audience of the 'heaven and the earth'. Although Israel did eventually rebel, and although she was banished into exile by God, the climax of the Song of Moses requires that God not abandon His people entirely. And the creation is God's witness to that promise! So then, on the basis of that covenant witness alone, God must keep His word. In effect, creation is God's guarantor.

---

[22] Thomas Keiser. "The Song of Moses: A Basis for Isaiah's Prophecy." Vetus Testamentum 55.4 (2005): 489-90.

Isaiah 49:6, 8-9

> It is too light a thing that you should be my servant to raise up the tribes of Jacob and to bring back the preserved of Israel; **I will make you as a light for the nations, that my salvation may reach to the end of the earth**. … Thus says the LORD: In a time of favor I have answered you; in a day of salvation I have helped you; **I will keep you and give you as a covenant to the people**, to establish the land, to apportion the desolate heritages, saying to the prisoners, 'Come out,' to those who are in darkness, 'Appear.' **They shall feed along the ways; on all bare heights shall be their pasture.**'

We see that it is not enough for God to simply make good on the original terms of His covenant. No! According to God, that is 'too light a thing.' The prophet says to 'my servant', which is Christ, 'I will make you as a light for the nations, that my salvation may reach the end of the earth'. Not only does God intend to save the remnant of His people, but also He intends to expand His reach to all nations. The terms of this covenant have been dramatically changed.

But who will be a witness to this new covenant? 'Give ear, O heavens, and I will speak, and let the earth hear the words of my mouth'. God's universe, His creation alone, is the only possible witness that He can provide. It was to the creation that God spoke, through Moses, when He predicted the latter end of His first covenant with Israel. And so it is to the creation once more that God must look, for a witness of His new covenant, which was His plan to include Gentiles in Jewish promises.

Since creation is everything, so to speak, it seems logical that all people should be given opportunity to follow God. This is a key principle in Isaiah's creation commentary, and explains why Genesis 1 does not use the personal name of Adam in reference to human creation. Human beings are presented in a universal sense. So then it is Isaiah who borrows heavily from the Song of Moses, and it is Isaiah who focuses Israel's attention back to the text of Genesis 1.

We should realize that the literal, physical heaven could not 'give ear', or listen, as Moses demanded. Neither could the literal physical coastlands 'listen', or 'give attention', as Isaiah demanded. The literal, physical heaven, earth, and mountains cannot even 'rejoice' or 'sing' with Israel when God ultimately fulfills His promises to the Gentile believers. When God speaks to the objects of creation after this manner, He is speaking symbolically to nations of believers irrespective of their physical heritage. By extension, He is predicting their future existence, for these nations of believers did not yet exist. This explains why Genesis 1 is the only Biblical creation text which describes God speaking to inanimate objects during the process of creation.

Of course, this creation symbolism is confirmed by Paul in the NT, who takes his cue from Moses and Isaiah. Among other passages, Paul quotes the Song of Moses and interprets the term 'heaven' to represent the 'nations', or future believers of all nationalities.[23, 24]

---

[23] Deut. 32:43; Romans 15:10

[24] It should be noted that the KJV translation of Deut. 32:43 is demonstrably lacking, as are all other translations based primarily on the Masoretic Text (MT). Both the Septuagint (LXX) and Dead Sea Scrolls (DSS) contain the phrase 'Rejoice with him, O heavens', rather than the phrase 'Rejoice, ye nations'. Since both the LXX and the DSS predate the MT by many centuries, most modern translations prefer the reference to the 'heaven'. This decision is supported, for example, by the parallel passages in Deutero-Isaiah which also use the word 'heaven'. And Hebrews 1:6 confirms for us that the LXX and DSS are the more accurate variants of Deut 32:43. The author of Hebrews cites 'Let all the angels of God worship him', as found in the LXX and DSS, which quote is also missing from Deut. 32:43 in the MT.

The point is that Isaiah does correlate the 'heavens' with the 'nations'. So then Paul does the same. He references the term 'heaven' from the LXX version of Deut 32:43, being the extant Greek manuscript of his day, and changes it to ἔθνος (ethnos) (nations) in Romans 15:10. This is an *interpretation*, and not a correction. He substitutes one word for the other, to convey a spiritual principle, on authority from the OT. He lists the modified quote among several other OT passages referring to nations of believers. This makes sense, in that the Song of Moses is explicitly address to the 'heaven' and the 'earth', and refers to the 'heaven' multiple times in its opening lines. It is completely appropriate therefore that it also refer to the 'heaven' in its conclusion.

Paul also quotes Isaiah in that same chapter, when he states 'Those **who have never been told** of him will see, and those **who have never heard** will understand.'[25] Here again is Paul's exposition of that 'mystery hidden from the beginning'. 'For I tell you that Christ became a servant to the circumcised to show God's truthfulness, in order to confirm the promises given to the patriarchs, **and in order that the Gentiles might glorify God for his mercy.'**[26]

Revelation 15:2-4

'And I saw what appeared to be a sea of glass mingled with fire—and also those who had conquered the beast and its image and the number of its name, standing beside the sea of glass with harps of God in their hands. And they **sing the song of Moses**, the servant of God, and the song of the Lamb, saying, 'Great and amazing are your deeds, O Lord God the Almighty! Just and true are your ways, **O King of the nations**! Who will not fear, O Lord, and glorify your name? For you alone are holy. **All nations will come and worship** you, **for your righteous acts have been revealed.**'

The Song of Moses is revived once more, at the end of the Bible, by the prophet John. For indeed, the creation theme of Moses, Isaiah, and Paul is the greatest prophetic revelation of all time. 'All nations will come and worship' the 'King of the nations'. This further correlates the 'heavens' of Moses with the 'nations' of Isaiah and the NT.

So why does the MT read 'nations' instead of 'heaven'? Dr. Tigay surmises that later Jewish rabbis, when copying the MT, changed the term 'heaven' to 'nations' in order to preclude the inference that supernatural beings existed in the 'heaven' which should be worshiped. See Jeffrey Tigay, *The JPS Torah Commentary: Deuteronomy: The Traditional Hebrew Text with the New JPS Translation*, (Philadelphia: Jewish Publication Society, 1996), pgs. 314, 514-518. Ironically, this rabbinical alteration of the MT in the medieval period mirrors Paul's previous change in the first century, minus the critical, symbolic connection.

[25] Romans 15:21
[26] Romans 15:8-9

We have thus established the non-literal function of the spiritual mystery of Genesis 1. We have established a literary precedent whereby creation is witness to a new and audible covenant which intended to convey God's future plans for all people. Creation itself is evidence of the covenant, and creation itself will hold God to His word. So then creation represents people, and creation represents what God intends to do with those people. The 'former' or old covenant was highlighted by the Song of Moses, and the 'new' covenant was highlighted by Genesis 1. This is what Isaiah teaches Israel. When we say that Genesis 1 has a non-literal function in Scripture, this is precisely what we mean. How fitting! How ironic! The most sacred of Jewish scriptures, that is the first five books of the OT, begin with the new covenant creation witness of Genesis 1 and end with the old covenant witness of Duet. 32.

III. The Parables Of Creation

Genesis 1 is directly associated with parables, both in the OT and the NT. All of these parables require explanation, and function to reveal God's covenant with all nations.

Christ recalled with disgust Isaiah's words during his own ministry, and recognized that Israel could not accept him for who he really was. He told his disciples, 'Unto you it is given to know **the mystery of the kingdom of God**: but unto them that are without, **all these things are done in parables**: That seeing they may see, and not perceive; and hearing they may hear, and not understand; lest at any time they should be converted, and their sins should be forgiven them.'[27] This veil upon Israel applied to many aspects of the OT scriptures[28], and necessarily included the text of Genesis 1. Deutero-Isaiah reveals to us that Israel did not understand the spiritual meaning of that text. And despite the attempts to rectify that circumstance, the vast majority of God's audience did not embrace His intentions for other nations of believers.

So then Paul's description of the creation as a 'mystery' is entirely appropriate. And by extension, one might equally refer to the creation as a parable. But this new description may be both surprising and disturbing for some, because they do not feel comfortable equating creation 'from the beginning' with the stories that Jesus used to teach the Jews in the gospels. In reality, however, this comparison is accurate. A mystery is simply that which cannot be understood plainly, or at first glance. It requires specific effort and assistance, to make the mystery known. In similar vein, it is imperative that we understand what exactly a parable is, and how it is used in Scripture.[29]

---

[27] Mark 4:11-12
[28] Romans 11:7-10; II Cor. 3:12-16
[29] See Appendix IV. What Is A Parable?

The parable genre is both complex and yet, in another sense, spectacularly simple. The reader should recognize that Biblical parables often utilize literal objects and concepts for comparison, whether actually based on literal events or not. For example, when Jesus speaks of the Sower and the Seed, he is not referring to seeds planted in the ground at all. He says so himself. 'The seed is the Word of God.'[30] He is making a comparison to something literal, but his words are very obviously non literal. The point here is that without Divine guidance, it is impossible to understand the spiritual meaning of any parable. If a text is a parable then the plain reading is incomplete. We still require the spiritual meaning of any parable to be revealed to us.

And so a parable is composed of two aspects. First, a parable has a source, which may or may not be based on literal events. Second, a parable has an application, or meaning, which is compared to the source. In some instances, the application of a Biblical parable is included alongside the source text. This is more than convenient; it is essential. It is God's meaning, and not ours. In other instances, some aspect or portion of a parable may be so obvious as to be interpreted by widespread consensus without any significant effort. In the absence of these, however, the application of a parable may be made known by another Biblical author entirely.

Once we understand the full scope of the term 'parable', we recognize that this popular Biblical genre coincides precisely with Isaiah's commentary on Genesis 1. Genesis 1 does contain a spiritual meaning 'from the beginning', which is revealed in both the OT and the NT. This proposition necessarily invokes symbolic comparison, and so the sole requirement for an OT parable has been met. It would be absurd for the Christian to propose that God did not plan to include all nations in Jewish promises from the moment of creation. The fact that God predicted His future covenant in symbolic format is merely the logical outworking of the principle, which Isaiah has made clear.

Matthew 13:10-12, 34-35

---

[30] Luke 8:11

'Then the disciples came and said to him, 'Why do you speak to them in parables?' And he answered them, '**To you it has been given to know the secrets of the kingdom of heaven, but to them it has not been given.** For to the one who has, more will be given, and he will have an abundance, but from the one who has not, even what he has will be taken away'. ... All these things Jesus said to the crowds in parables; indeed, **he said nothing to them without a parable. This was to fulfill what was spoken by the prophet: 'I will open my mouth in parables; I will utter what has been hidden since the foundation of the world.'**

Following a series of parables, the gospel writer declares by way of quotation that Jesus' teaching method was a specific fulfillment of Psalm 78. He declares that Jesus' parables actually teach concepts that were 'hidden since the foundation of the world'. Surely this cannot be mere coincidence? This mimics the language of Isaiah and Paul. This is *their* characteristic description of creation as a witness to God's global covenant, and merits further investigation.

Psalm 78:1-11, 67-70

'A Maskil of Asaph. **Give ear, O my people, to my teaching; I will open my mouth in a parable; things that we have heard and known, that our fathers have told us. I will utter dark sayings from of old, incline your ears to the words of my mouth!** We will not hide them from their children, but tell to the coming generation the glorious deeds of the LORD, and his might, and the wonders that he has done. He established a testimony in Jacob and **appointed a law in Israel, which he commanded our fathers to teach to their children, that the next generation might know them,** the children yet unborn, and arise and tell them to their children, so that they should set their hope in God and not forget the works of God, but keep his commandments; and that they should not be like their fathers, a stubborn and rebellious generation, a generation whose heart was not steadfast, whose spirit was not faithful to God. **The Ephraimites**, armed with the bow, turned back on the day of battle. **They did not keep God's covenant,** but refused to walk according to his law. **They forgot his works and the wonders**

> that he had shown them. … **He rejected the tent of Joseph; he did not choose the tribe of Ephraim, but he chose the tribe of Judah**, Mount Zion, which he loves. He built his sanctuary **like the high heavens, like the earth, which he has founded forever. He chose David his servant** and took him from the sheepfolds.'

We may observe several literary similarities between the opening lines of the Maskil of Asaph[31] and the Song of Moses in Duet. 32, which was discussed previously. Asaph models his text after Moses, using three themes as follows.

THE SONG OF MOSES	THE MASKIL OF ASAPH
Give ear, O heavens, and I will speak, and let the earth **hear the words of my mouth** - Deut 32:1	**Give ear,** O my people, to my teaching; **incline your ears to the words of my mouth** - Psalm 78:1
Remember the days of old; consider the years of many generations; **ask your father, and he will show you,** your elders, and **they will tell you.** - Deut 32:7	..things that we have heard and known, **that our fathers have told us.** - Psalm 78:3
Take to heart all the words by which I am warning you today, **that you may command them to your children**, that they may be careful to do all the words of this law. - Duet 32:46	**We will not hide them from their children,** but tell to the coming generation...He established a testimony in Jacob and appointed a law in Israel, **which he commanded our fathers to teach to their children** - Psalm 78:4-5

Table 4: The Maskil Of Creation

---

[31] Just as in the case of Isaiah, the author here attributes Psalm 78 to one man named Asaph for sake of convenience. There is textual evidence which might contradict this conclusion, but this does not affect our study.

First, Asaph opens with an explicit demand for the attention of his audience. Second, he proclaims that his words were known by previous generations. Third, he reiterates the command of Moses which required the older generations to teach the younger generations so that they would not forget God's principles. The use of these themes is a deliberate attempt by Asaph to draw the reader back in mind to the Song of Moses. It is entirely appropriate therefore that Asaph would also do this using *musical* liturgy.

Asaph seeks to remind Israel of their rebellious tendencies. He cites a specific set of examples from their own national history, as justification for a Divine principle. Asaph sets Ephraim against Judah[32], and explains that one was rejected because 'they did not keep God's covenant', while the other was accepted because they 'set their hope in God and [did] not forget the works of God, but kept His commandments.' This division between God's own people is represented at the conclusion of the psalm by the choice of David as king, and subsequently by the messianic promises given to David and his family line.

The Song of Moses had already predicted the national rebellion of Israel, and so Asaph follows its literary pattern because he provides evidence of its fulfillment. The events leading up to the selection of David as king are a relevant OT example of God's plan to include

---

[32] 'Since 'Ephraim' was a specific tribe of Israel, careful contextual analysis should be used when distinguishing the differences in *tribal* and *figurative kingdom* identifications within the Tanakh, especially since the Prophets used the terms 'Ephraim', 'Joseph', and 'Israel' interchangeably, speaking of the same entity, the Northern Kingdom of Israel, the House of Israel, or the House of Joseph. Zechariah 10:6

'Judah', likewise was a name used for both a *tribe* and *kingdom* (the tribe of Judah, the Kingdom of Judah, the House of Judah, and even the House of David (King David being a descendant of Judah)).

To see where 'Ephraim' and 'Judah' are used in this idiomatic fashion within the Hebrew Scriptures, see Isaiah 7:17,9:21,11:13; Hosea 5:5,5:12-14,6:4,10:11,11:12; Ezekiel 37:16-19; Zechariah 9:13,10:6.' See Wikipedia contributors. "Ephraim and Judah." *Wikipedia, The Free Encyclopedia*. Wikipedia, The Free Encyclopedia, 29 Mar. 2014. Web. 3 Mar. 2015.

Gentiles in Jewish promises. King David's own band of 'mighty men' included many Gentile warriors, who fought with courage for both David and the God of Israel.[33] As a result of their faithfulness, these Gentiles were loved and respected by David. They receive, in effect, the commendation of God above even those natural Israelites who were not similarly dedicated to the truth. David's Gentile band of 'mighty men' was not like the tribe of Ephraim, who 'turned back on the day of battle!'

So then, Asaph's own description of his Maskil is quite accurate. 'I will open my mouth in a parable…I will utter dark sayings from קֶדֶם (qedem) (ancient time).' Previously, Isaiah outlined for us several different key words in connection with God's creation of the earthly and heavenly structures in Genesis 1. In particular, we may recall the word (qedem), meaning 'ancient time'. Now Asaph also speaks of this לְמָשָׁל (mashal) (MT) or παραβολή (parabolē) (LXX) from (qedem) ancient time. And Matthew confirms for us that Asaph intends (qedem) to refer to the καταβολή κόσμος (katabolē kosmos) (the foundation of the world).[34] With the impact of this connection, the Maskil of Asaph springs to life like never before.

But let us be very clear. What is the parable, and from where does it come? The parable is God's plan to include Gentiles in Jewish promises. It is revealed by Isaiah's extensive commentary on Genesis 1. This parable is elsewhere referred to by Paul as the 'mystery hid from the beginning', and by Asaph as the 'parable from ancient time'. The parable was 'hidden', merely because its revelation was rejected by the ancient audience. And the parable was 'from the beginning', because its source is the text which corresponds to the very 'beginning' of all things, or the creation of

---

[33] II Samuel 23:8-38

[34] Although Matthew's text is written in Greek, his phrase (katabolē kosmos) is not a direct quote of Psalm 78 from the LXX. The LXX instead has the word ἀρχή (archē) (origin), which is often used in both the OT and the NT to refer to the *very* beginning of creation. (Archē) is also used in several instances in the LXX translation of Isaiah 40-66, with respect to the creation of the heaven and the earth. This reinforces for us the fact that the text of Genesis 1 is the specific source of the parable which reveals God's plan to include Gentiles in Jewish promises. Although (katabolē) and (archē) do not carry precisely the same meaning, it remains possible to use them interchangeably at least in this context.

the heaven and the earth. This is verified repeatedly by the imagery used throughout Scripture to communicate the parable.

And Jesus' use of parables to hide the exposition of his teaching stems directly from this point. Recall that the text of Genesis 1 was separated from Isaiah's enlightening commentary, specifically because God knew that Israel was a 'rebel from the womb'[35]. Similarly, since Israel did not accept God's right to choose His own people, and did not recognize the requirements of faith which extended even to Gentiles, they were not permitted to understand the teachings of Jesus. The vast majority of those who heard his parables were consumed with pride in their national heritage.

Notice carefully the repeated theme in each of Jesus' parables, as recorded in Matthew 13. The parable of the Sower and the Seed, the parable of the Weeds, the parable of the Mustard Seed, the parable of Leaven, the parable of the Hidden Treasure, the parable of the Pearl of Great Price, and the Parable of the Net all deal with specific aspects of the Divine process by which God will ultimately establish His kingdom. It is indeed a slow process, starting very small at first, and focused on spreading God's message to as many as will hear. The process eventually culminates with the final examination and division of the faithful believers from the unfaithful. Those who are judged worthy, such as the good Seed, the Wheat, and the good Fish, will ultimately be people of any race or nationality. And the choice of Judah over Ephraim, in the Maskil of Asaph, is a microcosm of this kingdom process. The Jews in the first century had become like Ephraim of old. They had refused to consider God's right to choose on His own basis, the basis of faith.

The opening line of the Maskil of Asaph was thus a declaration of Asaph's intent to communicate a set of spiritual principles which affected others besides the Jewish people. And the author of Matthew was inspired to connect this OT intent with Christ. Many of the Jews could not bear to consider the evidence from their own history, and admit that their nation alone did not hold exclusive rights to the favor of God. Jesus said, 'I tell you, there were many widows in Israel in the days of Elijah, when the heavens were shut up three years and six months, and a great famine came over all the

---

[35] Isaiah 48:3-8

land, and Elijah was sent to none of them but only to Zarephath, in the land of Sidon, to a woman who was a widow. And there were many lepers in Israel in the time of the prophet Elisha, and none of them was cleansed, but only Naaman the Syrian.' When they heard these things, all in the synagogue were filled with wrath.'[36]

It turns out that this Divine, multi-national kingdom model, with its roots in creation, is not a concept isolated to Matthew 13. It is rather only one of many similar references to creation scattered throughout the NT. The parable of the Good and Faithful Servant also follows this model. It expressly defines for us that the reward for the faithful, which is an inheritance in the future kingdom of God, was 'prepared **from the foundation of the world**'.[37] Jesus Christ looked forward to the time when his disciples would be with him in the kingdom because, as he says to his Father, 'you loved me **before the foundation of the world**.'[38] Paul also indicates that Genesis 1 is a discourse on the Divine plan for all believers. He explains God's process in these same terms. 'He chose us in Him **before the foundation of the world**.'[39] Peter declares that Jesus himself was 'foreknown **before the foundation of the world**',[40] and John agrees with Paul when he states that all believers are 'written **before the foundation of the world** in the book of life of the Lamb.'[41]

Obviously, something very important must have happened at the (katabolē kosmos) (the foundation of the world). Taken individually, however, it is easy to oversimplify these statements without considering their significant weight. These are *not* merely references to the fact that God knew within Himself the outcome of future events at the time of creation. Such a conclusion is, by comparison, elementary and completely undermines all of the Biblical witnesses we have reviewed thus far.

---

[36] Luke 4:25-28
[37] Matthew 25:34
[38] John 17:24
[39] Ephesians 1:4
[40] I Peter 1:20
[41] Revelation 13:8; 17:8

Under normal circumstances, when an individual wishes to hide something, he or she makes no mention of it whatsoever. They keep it to themselves. However, this is not what God intended at all. God did not hide certain concepts 'from the beginning' by simply keeping His mouth shut. Isaiah's commentary on Genesis 1 reveals specific, spiritual imagery relevant to believers of all nationalities, which was subsequently ignored by the vast majority of the OT Jewish audience.

So then Jesus' own preferred teaching method is exemplary of this distinction. While often hiding his meaning with the use of parables, he nevertheless spoke openly. He did not keep his mouth shut completely; he did not 'hide' the meaning in that sense. He simply withheld the necessary spiritual commentary from all but a select few. It would be impossible for believers to understand and agree upon the 'literal' meaning of Christ's parables, without further explanation. And that is precisely what we see with the spiritual function of Genesis 1.

There should now be no reasonable objection to the characterization of Genesis 1 as a parable. The parables of Jesus, as defined by the gospel of Matthew, provide explicit confirmation of this view. They are the same teachings as those 'hidden since the foundation of the world'. In fact, the Divine requirement to selectively hide the spiritual function of creation was the impetus for the parable genre in the first place. The use of creation as a new covenant witness is blindingly obvious, but only after it has been shown to us.

IV.   The Sabbath Of Creation

Genesis 1 portrays a sequence of days which mimics the literal Sabbath cycle. But this specific relationship is based on literary similarity, rather than literal equivalence.

Both Isaiah and Paul reveal to us that Genesis 1 should represent a timeline of covenant events, whereby the Gentiles might be included in Jewish promises. So then it should come as no surprise, when we see that Genesis 1 does form a deliberate sequence. More specifically, it is a sequence of literal days.

This is fully supported by the basic grammar of the text. The use of the word יוֹם (yowm) (day) in Hebrew always refers to a literal, 24 day when used in conjunction with a numerical adjective, i.e. the 'first day'.[42] While some modern lay scholars have attempted to dispute this conclusion[43], the expert linguistic opinion is and always has been unanimous. Dr. James Barr, the highly distinguished Professor of Hebrew at Oxford University, stated very clearly the plain meaning of the days of creation from a textual perspective alone.

---

[42] 'The exegetical evidence suggests the word 'day' in this chapter refers to a literal twenty-four hour day. It is true that the word can refer to a longer period of time (see Isa 61:2, or the idiom in 2:4, 'in the day,' that is, 'when'). But this chapter uses 'day,' 'night,' 'morning,' 'evening,' 'years,' and 'seasons.' Consistency would require sorting out how all these terms could be used to express ages. Also, when the Hebrew word יוֹם (yom) is used with a numerical adjective, it refers to a literal day. Furthermore, the commandment to keep the Sabbath clearly favors this interpretation. One is to work for six days and then rest on the seventh, just as God did when he worked at creation.' See the NET Bible notes, Gen. 1:5
[43] Rodney Whitefield, 'The Hebrew Word 'Yom' Used With A Number in Genesis 1', 2006,
<http://godandscience.org/youngearth/yom_with_number.pdf> (10 Feb 2015).

'Probably, so far as I know, there is no professor of Hebrew or Old Testament at any world-class university who does not believe that the writer(s) of Genesis 1–11 intended to convey to their readers the idea that creation took place in a series of six days which were the same as the days of 24 hours we now experience. ... Or, to put it negatively, the apologetic arguments which suppose the 'days' of creation to be long eras of time ... are not taken seriously by any such professors, as far as I know.'[44]

Dr. Harlow, Professor of Religion at Calvin College concurs when he states,

'The days pictured in Genesis 1 are **regular, twenty-four-hour periods of time**. It simply will not do to suggest that they are 'really' long geological epochs, as in the so-called day-age theory. Nor will it do to posit a gap of billions of years between verse 1 and verse 2 or verse 3, as in the so called gap theory, in order to harmonize Genesis 1 with our modern knowledge that the earth is billions of years old. **The ancient Israelite author and his audience had no notion of geological ages**, which is a distinctly modern concept, and not a clue that the universe is as old as mainstream science has shown it to be, some 13.7 billion years by the latest reckoning. More pertinently, though, the repeated phrase 'evening and morning' indicates clearly that these are normal, twenty-four-hour days. **That is how the text pictures them**.'[45]

And yet, neither Dr. Barr nor Dr. Harlow assert that God actually created the literal heaven and earth in one literal week. Using the same logic, for example, we should be able to prove conclusively that Jesus' use of the word 'seed' in the parable of the Sower and the Seed refers to a literal seed planted in the ground. Point in fact, that is the only meaning the grammar can convey, and yet it remains a demonstrably wrong interpretation.

[44] James McGrath, 'Mined Quote from James Barr', 23 Aug 2012, <http://www.patheos.com/blogs/exploringourmatrix/2012/08/mined-quote-from-james-barr.html> (10 Feb 2015).
[45] Daniel Harlow, 'Creation According to Genesis: Literary Genre, Cultural Context, Theological Truth' *Christian Scholar's Review* 37 (2008): 177. Emphasis mine.

The study of grammar is important, but alone it can never solve all our exegetical problems. In the case of Jesus' parable, the literal word 'seed' actually represents the 'Word'. And we might just as easily take the Lord Jesus Christ at his literal word where he states 'Go and tell that fox, 'Behold, I cast out demons and perform cures **today and tomorrow, and the third day** I finish my course. Nevertheless, I must go on my way **today and tomorrow and the day following**, for it cannot be that a prophet should perish away from Jerusalem.'[46]   Christ's use of the phrase 'third day' as a time period in Luke 13 was not to be taken in the plain sense. And this is only made known to us, with the benefit of hindsight. So while it is true that the words on the page of Genesis 1 do convey literal, 24 hour days, that is not the end of the matter.

No reasonable Bible student can draw any dogmatic conclusion about the literal or nonliteral basis of any portion of Scripture in isolation, when additional evidence exists to be considered. This may come in the form of positive evidence, whereby another passage affirms a particular concept in plain literal terms. But this may also come in the form of negative evidence, whereby another passage presents a symbolic or metaphorical perspective.

Exodus 31:13; 16-17

> 'You are to speak to the people of Israel and say, 'Above all **you shall keep my Sabbaths, for this is a sign between me and you** throughout your generations, **that you may know that I, the LORD, sanctify you.** ... Six days shall work be done, but the seventh day is a Sabbath of solemn rest, holy to the LORD. Whoever does any work on the Sabbath day shall be put to death. Therefore the people of Israel shall keep the Sabbath, **observing the Sabbath throughout their generations, as a covenant forever. It is a sign forever between me and the people of Israel** that in six days the LORD made heaven and earth, and **on the seventh day** he rested and was refreshed.'

---

[46] Luke 13:32-33

According to this passage, the Sabbath represents God's covenant with Israel. It is important to note that this אוֹת ('owth) (sign, token) of the covenant is not restricted solely to the seventh day of rest. Rather, the 6 days of work are a vital component of the 'sign'. They are given equal mention in the passage. The people were instructed to work as God worked, and then rest as God rested. Thus all seven days of the week were reflected in Genesis 1, and by extension all seven days constitute the 'sign' of the covenant.

Psalm 92:1-2; 4-6

> 'A Psalm. **A Song for the Sabbath**. It is good to give thanks to the LORD, to sing praises to your name, O Most High; to declare your steadfast love **in the morning**, and your faithfulness **by night**, For you, O LORD, have made me glad by your work; at **the works of your hands** I sing for joy. **How great are your works, O LORD! Your thoughts are very deep!** The stupid man cannot know; **the fool cannot understand this**:'

Within the context of the Sabbath Day psalm, the Lord's work, that is the 'work' of His 'hands', can be none other than the creation itself. Notice the reference to the 'morning' and the 'evening'. Both the Sabbath cycle and now the Sabbath Day psalm reflect the six days of creative work God did in Genesis 1. Further, the psalmist connects God's 'works' with God's 'thoughts', or מַעֲשֶׂה (ma`aseh) (meditate, purpose, plot). This confirms a link between the 'works' of creation, and the future plans of God, which Isaiah and Paul have already established.

A ritual covenant sign, such as the Sabbath, stands as a representative image of an agreement between God and His followers. It is a cyclical observance, and it conveys a poignant meaning. But the Sabbath is not just another ordinary OT type. As it turns out, it is one of only three OT rituals that relate to the hidden, spiritual mystery of creation. These three are the sign of Circumcision, the sign of Passover, and the sign of the Sabbath. All three of these rituals are *very* unique. They stand apart from the rest of the OT spiritual types and shadows, for several reasons.

	PARTICIPATE	COMMEMORATE	OBSERVE	REPRESENT
CIRCUMCISION	Jews and male, Gentile slaves	Behold, my covenant is with you, and you shall be the father of a multitude of nations	Predates the law	You shall be circumcised in the flesh of your foreskins
PASSOVER	Jews and male, Gentile slaves	For he passed over the houses of the people of Israel in Egypt	Predates law	They shall take some of the blood and put it on the two doorposts and the lintel
SABBATH	All Jews and Gentiles of any gender or status	In six days the Lord made heaven and earth, and on the seventh day He rested s	Predates the law	Six days shall work be done, but the seventh day is a Sabbath of solemn rest

Table 5: OT Signs Of The Mystery

First, these three ritual covenant signs are relevant to the spiritual theme of the Gentiles precisely because special allowances are made upfront for Gentile participation. In the case of Circumcision and Passover, male slaves in Jewish households were allowed to participate.[47] In the case of Sabbath, gender and racial restrictions were removed entirely.[48] This universal aspect of the Sabbath sign is strongly emphasized by Isaiah's creation commentary[49], and suggests that the Sabbath sign was the most important of the three rituals.

Second, these three ritual covenant signs were specifically instituted by God to commemorate a past event which He had accomplished. This is not the normal way in which types are thought to operate. It is generally assumed that types point forward in time, and so they do. But these three OT rituals, and these three only, first point back to the past. It is God's plan to include Gentiles in Jewish promises that has been predicted 'from the beginning'. More specifically, God has predicted *the end* from the beginning'. This is, by definition, backwards and so we should not be surprised by this apparently wrong order. The Sabbath sign was revealed last of the three, and yet it points back to the very first event of all, which is creation.

Third, these three ritual covenant signs were all first observed prior to the giving of the law on Mt. Sinai.[50] This is significant. The technique used in the NT to legitimize Christianity as the natural progression of the Jewish law is to point to evidence which *predates* that law. God's plans to include Gentiles in Jewish promises were never an afterthought. This is the precise line of spiritual reasoning we see laid out by Paul.[51]

Finally, these three ritual covenant signs are not an exact copy of the thing which they attempt to represent. In fact, these types all follow the express principle of the representative image. The ritual signs

---

[47] Genesis 17:12, Exodus 12:44
[48] Exodus 20:10
[49] Isaiah 56:2-8
[50] The first Biblical record of Sabbath observance is 'the fifteenth day of the second month, after they had departed from the land of Egypt'. See Exodus 16:1, 23-26.
[51] Galatians 3:8, 17-19

themselves bear *no* literal equivalence with the acts of God which they commemorate. They only bear literary similarity. For example, the cutting off of the male foreskin represents division and separation. But circumcision of the people does *not* call to remembrance a physical circumcision performed upon God Himself. The same goes for Passover, where the blood over the doorposts does *not* call to remembrance a physical, ballistic trajectory by the angel of God overhead.

Only now that we have reviewed this related material, are we fully prepared to address the suggestion of literal creation days. It is quite often assumed, by virtue of the statements in Exodus, that the weekly Sabbath cycle proves the literal, physical creation also took place over the course of seven, 24 hour days. But when we examine the aforementioned details, as well as the Sabbath itself more closely, it should become evident that such a view makes no sense. This is supported by the following points.

SIGN	The Sabbath cycle is a spiritual sign of creation.
ACTIVITY	The creation days personify Divine activity.
DARKNESS	The seventh day of creation has no darkness.

Table 6: The Sabbath Of Creation

The presumption of literal creation days, on the basis of the Sabbath cycle, breaks the otherwise unanimous pattern of ritual covenant signs. Nowhere in Scripture do human beings commemorate their בְּרִית (bĕriyth) (covenant) with God by literally duplicating one another's representative images. The seven days of the Sabbath cycle *are* literal, 24 hour periods. They are also, by definition, a ritual covenant sign or type of the days of creation. We should not expect, therefore, that the creation days are literally identical to the 24 hour days of the week. The Sabbath cycle, by way of analogy, is rather the representative image of the creation days. And it is the days of creation which stand for the future fulfillment of God's promises to His people of all nationalities.

And yet, the references to 'six days' of creation found in Exodus 20:11 and 31:17 are still put forth as indisputable proof of the plain, literal days of creation. But again, are we still to confuse similarity with an exact replica? The mechanism of God's creative work is often described by Scripture in terms which would literally require physical activity utilizing physical body parts, as if God were a human. This type of imagery was already described in Psalm 92, the Sabbath day psalm. Elsewhere the psalmist states 'Of old you **laid the foundation** of the earth, and the heavens are **the work of your hands.**'[52] Again, '**My hand laid the foundation** of the earth, and my **right hand spread out** the heavens.'[53] In Exodus 31:17, the daily physical work performed by those in ancient Israel is compared with the creation, as if it too were Divine physical work. This is, by definition, anthropomorphism.[54] Strictly speaking, God did not perform any creative work with physical body parts in the plain literal sense.

And that's not all. As a result of God's apparently physical work of creation, the writer of Exodus insists that God subsequently stopped to 'catch breath' just as a normal human worker would do.[55] This

---

[52] Psalm 102:25

[53] Isaiah 48:13

[54] The medieval Jewish commentator Rashi notes regarding Exodus 31:17, 'He about Whom it is written: "He neither tires nor wearies" (Isa. 40:28), and Whose **every act is performed by speech [alone, without physical effort]**, dictated rest in reference to Himself [only] **in order to make it understood to the [human] ear with words that it can understand.**' Emphasis mine. See Rashi, '*Commentary on Exodus*', <http://www.chabad.org/library/bible_cdo/aid/9892#showrashi=true>. 10 March 2015.

[55] '**In this verse is a very bold anthropomorphism** in the form of the verb וַיִּנָּפַשׁ (vayyinnafash), a Niphal preterite from the root נָפַשׁ (nafash), the word that is related to 'life, soul' or more specifically 'breath, throat.' The verb is usually translated here as 'he was refreshed,' offering a very human picture. It could also be rendered '**he took breath**' (S. R. Driver, Exodus, 345). Elsewhere the verb is used of people and animals. The anthropomorphism is clearly intended to teach people to stop and refresh themselves physically, spiritually, and emotionally on this day of rest.' Emphasis mine. See the NET Bible Notes, Exodus 31:17.

too is anthropomorphism, and it makes perfect literary sense. Again, God is *not* merely portrayed in this case to speak creation into existence but rather to physically make it. So then neither the Divine work nor the Divine rest of God as described in Exodus is literally true in the plain sense. God did not actually do any physical work, nor did God actually stop to catch His breath, and yet that is precisely what the Hebrew text says.

The Divine work, the Divine rest, and the Divine time period of days are *all* equally important components of the Sabbath sign. And the first two components of the Sabbath sign are described in terms which are unequivocally anthropomorphic, i.e. not literally true in the plain sense. The *most* consistent conclusion therefore would be that the six day period of creation, as presented by the writer of Exodus, is similarly anthropomorphic.

The fact is that ancient peoples did not think of anthropomorphism as just another literary device. They did not generally conceive of higher order deities at all, without this type of phenomenological language.[56] Even today, any human description or account of God

---

[56] 'Based largely on myths, hymns, and prayers, scholars have traditionally understood Mesopotamian gods to be 'anthropomorphic, both externally and internally' (Van derToorn 2003:77) yet with 'gigantic size and ... superhuman powers' (Black / Green 1992:93), who populated a 'divine society [that] was as a replica of **human society**' (Roux 1964:88) albeit on a grander scale. ... **anthropomorphization of the major deities serves a practical purpose**. Ancient Mesopotamians naturally speculated about the nature of the world and their place in it. However, their musings were not merely philosophical abstractions; through them they sought to find meaning in their lives and in the world, to use all the powers available to succeed in a dangerous and volatile world. To do this, they strove to understand and approach the gods, perceived to be the ultimate sources of power and purpose. ... **Since many of the gods are understood primarily as human-like beings, humans may meaningfully communicate with them.** Since many of the gods are understood to be both comprehensible and approachable, their favor can be secured and their powers brought to bear on peoples' behalf. Likewise, **when humans are understood to be created in the image of the gods at least to some extent, they have greater dignity and a greater affinity to the gods. Thus, humanizing the divine is both unavoidable and profitable.** Although not all Mesopotamian deities are humanized, Mesopotamians

will require some type of accommodating language, but this was especially true in the ancient world. They purposefully blurred the lines between God, as portrayed for the purpose of human understanding, and God who 'is great, and **we know Him not**.'[57]

'Let no one pass judgment on you in questions of food and drink, or with regard to a festival or a new moon **or a Sabbath. These are a shadow of the things to come, but the substance belongs to Christ**.'[58] The sign of the literal seven day Sabbath cycle, like all the ritual observances of the OT, is as we have already said a σκιά (skia) (sketch, image, shadow). Anthropomorphism is an intentional feature of that shadow. It cannot be interpreted away, where the Biblical text presents it as necessary. Cumulatively, the literal work, the literal rest, and the literal days of the week were the shadow for the nation of Israel. They represent a rough comparison with the creation week, which cannot otherwise be made in precise detail.

And finally, we must also address the obvious parallel between the seventh day of rest in creation and the clear Biblical teaching that said day represents the kingdom age of the future. This future period is often referred to as the 'millenium', with a time span of 1,000 years.[59] The NT makes this connection without dispute.[60] However, it is this specific observation which further undermines the plain, literal argument for the creation days.

The seventh day of creation does not match the other days as described in Genesis 1. The precise repetition of the 'evening morning' refrain at the end of each day is deliberately omitted at the conclusion of creation, and this for a very important spiritual reason.

---

often appeal to the more humanized deities to deal with those that are less understandable and approachable, more primal and thus more dangerous.' Emphasis mine. See Michael B. Hundley, 'Here A God, There A God: An Examination of the Divine In Ancient Mesopotamia,' *Altorientalische Forschungen* 40 (2013): 72, 82-83.
<https://www.academia.edu/1162042/Here_a_God_There_a_God_Concept ions_of_Divinity_in_Ancient_Mesopotamia>.
[57] Job 36:26
[58] Colossians 2:16-17
[59] Revelation 20:4
[60] Hebrews 4:1-11

The seventh day has no darkness. 'Darkness' is one of four elements found at the beginning of Genesis 1, along with 'void', the lack of 'form', and the chaotic 'waters' of the 'deep', which all by definition are not 'good'. By the end of the text, however, all four of these conditions cannot be allowed to persist within the framework of the 'heaven and earth'.

On the first day, only the 'light' is referred to as 'good'. The darkness is obviously not good, and is explicitly isolated from said 'light'. It stems from the unacceptable conditions prior to creation, and so is left out of the commendation. Not until Day 4 do we find any light at all within the darkness, at which point the darkness is brought under subjection and 'ruled' over by the 'lesser' light. Although the darkness remains divided from the original light of Day 1, it now has another new light within itself. It is not completely dark any longer, but light mixed with dark, just as we see in the natural world. But that is not the end of the story. We have not yet reached the final conclusion. Day 7 is most important, not for what happens on that day, but rather for what does *not* happen on that day. God does not work, and there is no more 'evening morning' cycle.

The aforementioned parallel between creation and the kingdom age of the future makes this point very plain. In the future, '**The city has no need of sun or moon** to shine on it, **for the glory of God gives it light, and its lamp is the Lamb.... and there will be no night there**.'[61] And again, '**The sun shall be no more your light by day, nor for brightness shall the moon give you light**; but the LORD will be your everlasting light, and your God will be your glory. **Your sun shall no more go down, nor your moon withdraw itself**.'[62] Both of these passages explicitly relate to our spiritual context of Gentile believers. They also happen to correspond to the details of the seventh day of creation.

These passages, however, represent the spiritual conditions of life in the future, and are not to be taken as a plain literal description of the physical earth. The physical cycle of light and dark is critical to sustain life on earth as we know it, and the Bible teaches us this

---

[61] Revelation 21:23, 25
[62] Isaiah 60:19-20

same principle. 'While the earth remains, seedtime and harvest, cold and heat, summer and winter, **day and night, shall not cease.**'[63] So then the spiritual issue can be summarized by David where he states, 'even the darkness is not dark to you; **the night is bright as the day, for darkness is as light with you.**'[64] The seventh day of creation represents a principle that is compared with the physical concepts that we are familiar with, and ultimately reflects the spiritual conditions of the kingdom age.

Ultimately, our core premise is that the spiritual commentary on creation, revealed elsewhere, provides criteria by which we may better understand the plain source text. In this case, we should not expect to find reference to the seventh evening at all! And so we do not. It would contradict the predefined spiritual function of the text, no matter how we view its literal mechanics.

Therefore our modern literal understanding of the creation days is thus constrained by Scripture itself. This presents significant tension; it is no wonder that the creation timeline has been the subject of debate for thousands of years. When we over analyze the comparison between any Biblical sign and its source, from the modern perspective, it will inevitably break down. This is exactly what occurs when the belief in literal creation days is forced from the Sabbath sign.

We cannot conflate OT shadows with substance, simply because we cannot imagine the days of creation as anything other than plain literal days. We cannot avoid the nonliteral anthropomorphism of the Sabbath sign. We certainly cannot avoid the discrepancy which arises from the absence of darkness on the seventh day of creation.

If the plain reading of Genesis 1 is a modern, mechanical description of the physical creative process, then we should not expect to find any evidence to the contrary anywhere else in Scripture. Nevertheless we do find significant evidence, both here as described and elsewhere. The evidence indicates that the connection between the creation days and the Sabbath cycle is one of literary similarity. Genesis 1 follows the model of the Sabbath,

---

[63] Genesis 8:22
[64] Psalm 139:12

precisely because the Sabbath sign was established by God as the only OT ordinance which all nations where inherently free to participate in. This converges upon Isaiah's commentary on creation, which reveals Gods covenant plans for those same nations. We cannot presume that God actually worked for six literal days any more than we can presume that God literally built the creation with his hands, or was breathing hard by the time it was done. We should not ignorantly and inconsistently restrict ourselves to an apparently plain, literal text, and ignore all other Scriptural evidence and historical context to the contrary. [65]

---

[65] It is possible to interpret the days of creation as a series of inspired, 24 hour visions. This is a minority view, and is commonly known today as the 'Revelation Theory'. Given the consistent, parallel lines of evidence set forth here, however, these visions would still not represent a rigid, literal account of God's creative work in real time in the past. Only the visions themselves would have taken place in real time.

V.   The Symbols of Creation

Genesis 1 is explained by Scripture using interchangeable characters, which all follow a specific pattern. The purpose of these characters is to illustrate God's covenant with all nations in further detail.

Up until now, we have only seen God's covenant timeline revealed in outline form by the creation commentary of Deutero-Isaiah. So further review is necessary. Perhaps the symbols of Genesis 1 should be explicitly interpreted for us, in much greater detail.

To that end, the reader will recognize several different, interchangeable characters in the creation commentary which all carry the same basic spiritual meaning. These characters demand our attention. They represent both the 'former' things as well as the 'new' things of God's covenant timeline. Isaiah repeats the language of Genesis 1 and integrates all these characters to more fully reveal the details of His plan. In short, the 'new' creation is simply the 'old' creation reorganized with both new and recycled materials. Isaiah indicates that creation, from God's spiritual perspective, takes place in two phases, whereby the 'former' is destroyed in part and the 'new' arises from the ashes. And Genesis 1 represents the second phase, specifically because all nations are now included.

OLD JERUSALEM	TWO	CITIES	NEW JERUSALEM
• Bronze, Iron			• Gold, Silver
• Wood, Stone			• Bronze, Iron
• Gates Shut			• Gates Open
• Rebellion, Violence			• Salvation, Praise
DESOLATE WOMAN	TWO	WOMEN	**REMARRIED WOMAN**
• Unfaithful			• Faithful
• Sleeping			• Awake
• Divorced, Sold			• Redeemed Without Money
• Forgotten Children			• More Children
• Carried In Womb			• Carried After Birth
• Crying, Silence			• New Song, Shout for Joy
REVERSE CREATION	TWO	CREATIONS	**FORWARD CREATION**
• Old Heavens, Earth			• New Heavens, Earth
• Dry Up, Thirsty			• Springs, Pools
• Lay Waste			• Mountains, Trees, Plants
• Darkness, Blindness			• Universal Light
• Wild beasts			• Feed In Pasture
• Coastlands Wait, Hope			• Coastlands Hear, See

Table 7: The Symbols Of Creation

	THE CITY	THE WOMAN	THE CREATION
40:1-2,9-10,12-14	X	X	
41:2,10,17-20			X
42:1-2,5,9			X
42:10-17		X	X
43:18-21			X
44:1-4			X
44:21-28	X		X
45:1-2,7-8,10-12			X
46:3-5,9-13		X	
48:1-8	X		X
48:12-20			X
49:1-3,5-6,8-9,12-13			X
49:19-23		X	X
50:1-3		X	X
51:1-6			X
51:15-20	X	X	X
52:1-3,9-10	X	X	
54:1-8		X	
60:11-12,14,17-21	X		X
61:8-11		X	X
62:2-5,11-12	X	X	
65:16-19	X		X
66:1-2,7-14		X	X
66:18-22		X	X

Table 8: Isaiah's Commentary On Creation Symbols

Isaiah 40:1-2, 9-10, 12-14

> 'Comfort, comfort my people, says your God. Speak
> tenderly to Jerusalem, and **cry to her that her**
> **warfare is ended, that her iniquity is pardoned**, that
> she has received from the LORD's hand double for all
> her sins. ... Get you up to a high mountain, **O**
> **Zion**, herald of good news; lift up your voice with
> strength, **O Jerusalem**, herald of good news; lift it up,
> fear not; say to the cities of Judah, "Behold your God!"
> Behold, the Lord GOD comes with might, and his arm
> rules for him; behold, his reward is with him, and his
> recompense before him. ... **Who has measured the**
> **waters in the hollow of his hand and marked off the**
> **heavens with a span, enclosed the dust of the earth in**
> **a measure and weighed the mountains in scales and**
> **the hills in a balance**? Who has measured the Spirit of
> the LORD, or what man shows him his counsel? Whom
> did he consult, and who made him understand? Who
> taught him the path of justice, and taught him
> knowledge, and showed him the way of understanding?'

Isaiah repeatedly identifies the strength and intelligence of God,
which is manifest in His physical creation. He also compares that
creative ability with God's promise to forgive sins and save from
destruction in battle. This is relevant to our theme, of course, but
more importantly we now note the specific imagery that is
employed to make the point.

First, Israel is assigned a gender. 'Cry to **her**' says the prophet, and
again '**her** iniquity is pardoned. Second, this gender is equivocated,
in the collective sense, with the people of 'Jerusalem', 'Zion', and
even the 'cities of Judah'. So then we observe that Israel as a nation
can be represented as either a female, or a city, or both, as desired.
This format is pervasive throughout the OT, and Isaiah is
particularly fond of it.

Isaiah 41:2, 10, 17-20

> '**Who stirred up one from the east** whom victory meets
> at every step? **He gives up nations before him** ... **I will**
> **help you**...**When the poor and needy seek water**, and

there is none, and **their tongue is parched with thirst**, I the LORD will answer them; I the God of Israel will not forsake them. I will open rivers on the bare heights, and **fountains in the midst of the valleys**. I will make the **wilderness a pool of water**, and the **dry land springs of water**. I will put in the wilderness **the cedar, the acacia, the myrtle, and the olive**. I will set in the desert **the cypress, the plane and the pine together**, that they may see and know, may consider and understand together, that the hand of the LORD has done this, **the Holy One of Israel has created it.**'

Within the context of the 'one from the east' who 'will help', Isaiah overflows with creation imagery representing the salvation of God's people. Although the bodies of water and species of trees referred to already existed at the time the prophet spoke, they were completely irrelevant to the prophet's message. These particular trees and water sources will be אָרַב (bara') (created) in the future, for a special purpose.

And yet, the problems that faced Israel were not lack of water or shade. Isaiah describes the real problem in plain terms such as in verse 11 where he states 'all who are incensed against you shall be put to shame' and 'those who strive against you shall be as nothing'. This renders the literal, future creation of fountains, springs, pools and shade trees to be nonsensical. They would be of no help, and this is obvious. So then God is predicting His salvation of Israel with the use of creation imagery in a nonliteral sense. And this imagery is infused throughout Isaiah's commentary on Genesis 1. The problem of the people is posed in symbolic terms, i.e. 'poor' and 'parched', and so the solution similarly conforms to that literary perspective.

Isaiah 42:1-2, 5-9

'Behold my servant, whom I uphold, my chosen, in whom my soul delights; I have put my Spirit upon him; he will bring forth justice to the nations. He will not cry aloud or lift up his voice, or make it heard in the street … Thus says God, the LORD, who created the heavens and stretched them out, who spread out the

> **earth and what comes from it**, who gives breath to the
> people on it and spirit to those who walk in it: I am the
> LORD; **I have called you in righteousness**; I will take
> you by the hand and keep you; **I will give you as a
> covenant for the people, a light for the nations**, to
> open the eyes that are blind, to bring out the prisoners
> from the dungeon, from the prison those who sit in
> darkness. I am the LORD; that is my name; **my glory I
> give to no other**, nor my praise to carved idols. Behold,
> **the former things have come to pass**, and **new things I
> now declare; before they spring forth I tell you of
> them.**'

Up until this point, Isaiah has proclaimed the 'new' predictions of the future. The salvation of Israel is only made possible by the strength and foresight of the God who created the universe, and so Isaiah speaks boldly about the 'one from the east', or 'my servant whom I uphold'. It is in this 'chosen' one that God 'delights', and 'he will bring forth justice to the nations.' We acknowledge here a consistent theme concerning our Lord Jesus Christ. It is he who is undoubtedly the primary focus of the '*new things*' which Isaiah is compelled to reveal. It is he who is 'called', and it is he who represents 'a [new] covenant for the people, a light for [all] the nations.'

In contrast, Isaiah subsequently compares these 'new things' with the 'former things' predicted 'from the beginning'. Indeed, before Israel can be saved, she must first be put in a position which requires salvation. And before Israel can be put in that position, she must first exist! As we saw previously, the 'former things' involve the original creation of Israel 'from the womb', the 'appointment of the ancient people', her subsequent 'sin' and 'rebellion', and finally her temporary abandonment by God to the 'looter' and the 'plunderer'. [66] These had all 'come to pass' by the time Isaiah was prepared to declare 'new things before they spring forth'.

Isaiah 42:10-17

> '**Sing to the LORD a new song**, his praise from the end
> of the earth, you who go down to the sea, and all that fills

---

[66] Isaiah 42-43

it, the coastlands and their inhabitants. Let the desert and its cities **lift up their voice**, the villages that Kedar inhabits; let the habitants of Sela **sing for joy**, let them **shout from the top of the mountains**. Let them give glory to the LORD, and declare his praise in the coastlands. The LORD goes out like a mighty man, like a man of war he stirs up his zeal; he cries out, he shouts aloud, he shows himself mighty against his foes. For a long time I have held my peace; I have kept still and restrained myself; now **I will cry out like a woman in labor; I will gasp and pant. I will lay waste mountains and hills, and dry up all their vegetation; I will turn the rivers into islands, and dry up the pools. And I will lead the blind in a way that they do not know**, in paths that they have not known I will guide them. **I will turn the darkness before them into light**, the rough places into level ground. These are the things I do, and I do not forsake them. They are turned back and utterly put to shame, who trust in carved idols, who say to metal images, You are our gods.'

Here Isaiah describes the punishment of Israel prior to their salvation using the same type of creation imagery as found in chapter 41, but *in reverse*. 'I will *lay waste* mountains and hills, and *dry up* all their vegetation; I will turn the rivers into islands, and *dry up* the pools.' In parallel with that imagery, God is also described as if He was a 'woman in labor'. This echoes several passages elsewhere in Isaiah, which speak of God's plans for the nation as His child 'from the womb'. So then the symbolism shows us that the punishment of this child is actually part of the birth process.

However, the punishment of this child Israel does not result in complete destruction. The symbolic birth process is ultimately successful. Isaiah promises that God will 'lead the blind in a way that they do not know'. The final salvation of Israel is brought back into focus with creation imagery, as exhibited by the transition from 'darkness…into light', and Isaiah instructs his readers to incorporate *all* of these various types of imagery into a חֲדָשָׁה chadash (new) song for the 'end of the earth' and the 'coastlands'.

Isaiah 43:18-21

> 'Remember not the **former things**, nor consider the **things of old**. Behold, **I am doing a new thing; now it springs forth**, do you not perceive it? **I will make a way in the wilderness and rivers in the desert.** **The wild beasts will honor me**, the jackals and the ostriches, for **I give water in the wilderness**, rivers in the desert, to give drink to my chosen people, **the people whom I formed** for myself that they might declare my praise.'

The וִאשׁׁר (ri'shown) (former) things and the שָׁדָח chadash (new) things are continually emphasized by Isaiah, because they are of great importance. He positions himself precisely at the midway point of God's timeline, between these two series of events. Specific past events have not only been predicted, but also they have occurred. Now then, specific future events must also be predicted before they occur.

The past events are always characterized by the symbolic removal of moist conditions, leaving only dry conditions behind. The future events are always characterized by the symbolic restoration of moist conditions. Just as in the real world, spiritual water is a requirement of spiritual life.

Of particular interest here, the 'chosen people' are equivocated symbolically with the unclean animals of the law, such as 'wild beasts... the jackals and the ostriches.' And yet God promises they will 'honor me' as a result of the fact that they will drink of the 'water in the wilderness'. God also refers to these people more specifically with the language of creation. They are (yatsar) (formed) for His purposes.

Isaiah 44:1-4

> 'But now listen, O Jacob, my servant, Israel, whom I have chosen. This is what the LORD says-- **he who made you, who formed you in the womb, and who will help you**: Do not be afraid, O Jacob, my servant, Jeshurun, whom I have chosen. For **I will pour water on the thirsty land, and streams on the dry**

ground; I will pour out my Spirit on your offspring, and my blessing on your descendants. **They will spring up like grass in a meadow, like poplar trees by flowing streams.**'

Divine intervention is once more described like 'water on the thirsty land' of Israel. This water is equated with God's 'Spirit' whereby the people will 'spring up like grass…[and] poplar trees.' At the same time, this creation imagery is synonymous with a child רַצַי (yatsar) (formed) symbolically in God's 'womb'.

Isaiah 44:21-28

'**Remember these things**, O Jacob, and Israel, for you are my servant; **I formed you**; you are my servant; O Israel, you will not be forgotten by me. I have blotted out your transgressions like a cloud and your sins like mist; return to me, for I have redeemed you. **Sing, O heavens, for the LORD has done it; shout, O depths of the earth; break forth into singing**, O mountains, O forest, and every tree in it! For the LORD has redeemed Jacob, and will be glorified in Israel. Thus says the LORD, your Redeemer, **who formed you from the womb**: I am the LORD, **who made all things, who alone stretched out the heavens, who spread out the earth by myself,** who frustrates the signs of liars and makes fools of diviners, who turns wise men back and makes their knowledge foolish, who confirms the word of his servant and fulfills the counsel of his messengers, who says of **Jerusalem, She shall be inhabited, and of the cities of Judah, They shall be built**, and I will raise up their ruins; **who says to the deep, Be dry; I will dry up your rivers**; **who says of Cyrus, He is my shepherd, and he shall fulfill all my purpose**; saying of Jerusalem, She shall be built, and of the temple, Your foundation shall be laid.'

The reference to Cyrus as God's 'shepherd' provides us with an historical marker, and the writer obviously communicates at a time when Jerusalem is not actually inhabited. The return of the Jewish exiles from Babylon is a pivotal point in the history of God's people, to which the author looks forward to. From then on, 'new things' will 'spring forth', which eventually lead to Christ and the gospel preached to all nations. The creation is instructed to 'sing' and 'shout' in anticipation of this, because God who has (yatsar) (formed) Israel has also 'made all things…the heaven…the earth.'

Isaiah also reminds the people that God is sovereign over both the good and bad things that occur in their history. Not only will He 'build' and 'raise up their ruins', but also He 'says to the deep, by dry'. These are conflicting perspectives, which produce opposite results as desired. God makes use of both the good and the bad for His purposes.

Isaiah 45:1-2, 7-8, 10-12

> 'Thus says the LORD **to his anointed, to Cyrus, whose right hand I have grasped,** to subdue nations before him and to loose the belts of kings, to open doors before him that gates may not be closed: I will go before you and level the exalted places, I will break in pieces the doors of bronze and cut through the bars of iron … **I form light and create darkness, I make well-being and create calamity, I am the LORD,** who does all these things. **Shower, O heavens, from above, and let the clouds rain down righteousness; let the earth open, that salvation and righteousness may bear fruit; let the earth cause them both to sprout; I the LORD have created it.** … Woe to him who says to a father, What are you begetting? or to a woman, With what are you in labor? Thus says the LORD, the Holy One of Israel, and the one who formed him: **Ask me of things to come; will you command me concerning my children and the work of my hands?** I made the earth and created man on it; it was my hands that stretched out the heavens, and I commanded all their host. **I have stirred him up in righteousness,** and I will make all his ways level; **he shall build my city and set my exiles free, not for price or reward, says the LORD of hosts.'**

The impending redemption from Babylonian exile at present is again predicted by Isaiah, in parallel with several references to creation imagery. Light and darkness stand for prosperity and 'calamity', respectively, and represent both past and future events. Salvation and righteousness 'shower…from above', and subsequently 'sprout' and 'bear fruit'. Of course, these non-literal creation images make sense when we see that Isaiah explicitly equates His nation of 'children' with 'the work of my hands...the earth...the heavens.' So then *any* aspect of creation, whether it is water, plants, animals, humans, or even geographical features of the earth itself may be invoked as interchangeable spiritual symbols of God's covenant timeline for His people.

Isaiah 46:3-5, 9-13

'Listen to me, **O house of Jacob**, all the remnant of the house of Israel, **who have been borne by me from before your birth, carried from the womb**; even to your old age I am he, and to gray hairs I will carry you. **I have made, and I will bear; I will carry and will save.** ... Remember **the former things of old**; for I am God, and there is no other; **I am God, and there is none like me, declaring the end from the beginning and from ancient times things not yet done**, saying, 'My counsel shall stand, and I will accomplish all my purpose,' **calling a bird of prey from the east,** the man of my counsel from a far country. **I have spoken, and I will bring it to pass; I have purposed, and I will do it.** Listen to me, you stubborn of heart, you who are far from righteousness: I bring near my righteousness; it is not far off, and my salvation will not delay; I will put salvation in Zion, for Israel my glory.'

The gestational period of the child Israel in the womb of God is framed in very unnatural terms. It appears to continue even after the birth event! 'Even to your old age...and to gray hairs I will carry you,' says the prophet. This is important, because Israel is not like a normal child. In this symbolism, the full term of God's plan incorporates the final salvation of all nations. 'Carry' is equivocated with 'save', and Isaiah portrays the carrying process both before and after birth as equivalent.

Isaiah 48:1-8

'Hear this, **O house of Jacob**, who are called by the name of Israel, and who came from the waters of Judah, who swear by the name of the LORD and confess the God of Israel, but not in truth or right. **For they call**

> **themselves after the holy city**, and stay themselves on
> the God of Israel; the LORD of hosts is his name. **The
> former things I declared of old; they went out from
> my mouth, and I announced them; then suddenly I
> did them, and they came to pass**. Because I know
> that you are obstinate, and your neck is an iron sinew and
> your forehead brass, **I declared them to you from of
> old, before they came to pass I announced them to
> you**, lest you should say, My idol did them, my carved
> image and my metal image commanded them. You have
> heard; now see all this; and will you not declare it? **From
> this time forth I announce to you new things, hidden
> things that you have not known. They are created
> now, not long ago**; before today you have never heard of
> them, lest you should say, Behold, I knew them. **You
> have never heard, you have never known, from of old
> your ear has not been opened**. For I knew that you
> would surely deal treacherously, and that **from before
> birth you were called a rebel.**'

Israel, or the 'house of Jacob', wants to be identified as the people
of God. 'They call themselves after the holy city,' says Isaiah. This
echoes our earlier observation, wherein Israel as a whole is often
represented in Scripture as a city, e.g. Jerusalem. But Israel's
efforts fall short; they do not follow God 'in truth or right'.
Therefore, God declares that He has predicted this circumstance of
events 'before they came to pass'. He also equates the creation of
the world in the past with these predictions. Finally, God represents
His 'new things, hidden things' as if they were 'created now' as
opposed to 'long ago.' As noted, this is inspired metonymy which
links creation with spiritual predictions.

Isaiah 48:12-20

> 'Listen to me, O Jacob, and Israel, whom I called! I am
> he; I am the first, and I am the last. **My hand laid the
> foundation of the earth, and my right hand spread
> out the heavens**; when I call to them, they stand forth
> together. Assemble, all of you, and listen! **Who among
> them has declared these things**? The LORD loves
> him; he shall perform his purpose on Babylon, and his
> arm shall be against the Chaldeans. I, even I, have
> spoken and called him; I have brought him, and he will

prosper in his way. **Draw near to me, hear this: from the beginning I have not spoken in secret, from the time it came to be I have been there**. And now the Lord GOD has sent me, and his Spirit. Thus says the LORD, your Redeemer, the Holy One of Israel: I am the LORD your God, who teaches you to profit, who leads you in the way you should go. **Oh that you had paid attention to my commandments! Then your peace would have been like a river, and your righteousness like the waves of the sea**; your offspring would have been like the sand, and your descendants like its grains; their name would never be cut off or destroyed from before me. Go out from Babylon, flee from Chaldea, **declare this with a shout of joy**, proclaim it, send it out to the end of the earth; say, The LORD has redeemed his servant Jacob!'

Without question, the Babylonian exile was a terrible time in the history of Israel. It represented rock bottom, so to speak, for a nation filled with pride in their heritage. So then the prediction of their impending release is equally dramatic. 'Declare this with a shout of joy, proclaim it, send it out to the end of the earth!' But there is more. 'Draw near to me, hear this: from the beginning I have not spoken in secret, from the time it came to be I have been there!' God positions Himself as an active participant from initial prediction to final fulfillment, as we would expect.

The salvation of Israel is consistently interwoven with references to God and His creative abilities. And the focus remains on the text of Genesis 1. 'My hand laid the foundation of the earth, and my right hand spread out the heavens.' Isaiah tells us that God desires for Israel to have peace 'like a river, and…like the waves of the sea'. The imagery of water is always an integral component of the spiritual text.

Isaiah 49:1-3, 5-6, 8-9, 12-13

'**Listen to me, O coastlands, and give attention, you peoples from afar. The LORD called me from the womb**, from the body of my mother he named my name. He made my mouth like a sharp sword; in the shadow of his hand he hid me; he made me a polished arrow; in his quiver he hid me away. And he said to me, "You are my servant, Israel, in whom I will be glorified. … And now

> the LORD says, **he who formed me from the womb to be his servant**, to bring Jacob back to him; and that Israel might be gathered to him-- for I am honored in the eyes of the LORD, and my God has become my strength-- he says: It is too light a thing that you should be my servant to raise up the tribes of Jacob and to bring back the preserved of Israel; **I will make you as a light for the nations, that my salvation may reach to the end of the earth**. … Thus says the LORD: In a time of favor I have answered you; in a day of salvation I have helped you; **I will keep you and give you as a covenant to the people**, to establish the land, to apportion the desolate heritages, saying to the prisoners, 'Come out,' to those who are in darkness, 'Appear.' **They shall feed along the ways; on all bare heights shall be their pasture** … Behold, these shall come from afar, and behold, these from the north and from the west, and these from the land of Syene. **Sing for joy, O heavens, and exult, O earth; break forth, O mountains, into singing!** For the LORD has comforted his people and will have compassion on his afflicted.'

Although this passage has already been discussed, with respect to the Song of Moses, there remains additional imagery which should also be noted.

Our Lord Jesus Christ is depicted as a 'servant…formed from the womb.' This is similar to the imagery which depicts the childlike nation of Israel as a whole, except that Israel was 'called a rebel…from before birth.' The reference to a 'light for the nations' is obviously drawn from creation as well; it represents a new 'covenant'. Finally, and most unusual, is the fact that these people will 'feed along the way' and 'bare heights shall be their pasture'. This is imagery which is fitting for animals, rather than humans in the plain literal sense. It corresponds to the pattern of nonliteral creation imagery employed by Isaiah for many chapters.

Isaiah 49:19-23

> '**Surely your waste and your desolate places and your devastated land**-- surely now you will be too narrow for your inhabitants, and those who swallowed you up will be far away. **The children of your bereavement will**

> yet say in your ears: 'The place is too narrow for me;
> make room for me to dwell in.' Then you will say in
> your heart: **'Who has borne me these? I was bereaved
> and barren, exiled and put away, but who has
> brought up these? Behold, I was left alone; from
> where have these come**?' Thus says the Lord GOD:
> 'Behold, **I will lift up my hand to the nations**, and raise
> my signal to the peoples; and **they shall bring your sons
> in their bosom, and your daughters shall be carried
> on their shoulders. Kings shall be your foster fathers,
> and their queens your nursing mothers.**'

The prophet now introduces a twist on the imagery that has been
utilized up to this point. God is talking to Israel, about Israel. She
has previously been described as a child 'from the womb', but now
she is portrayed as a barren mother. Her condition is nonsensical in
the plain sense. It is not reasonable for any mother to suggest that
they did not have any children, when in fact they do. 'Who has
borne me these? I was bereaved and barren'. This observation is
highly instructive.

The land is described as 'waste and desolate' since, as you may
recall, reverse creation is the nonliteral imagery of choice with
regard to the anger and punishment of God. Israel, as a mother, has
been 'exiled and put away.' So then she will be very surprised
when the nations carry back her 'sons…and daughters…on their
shoulders.' 'From where have these come'? Israel will have so
many children, in fact, that 'they will yet say in your ears, 'The
place is too narrow for me'. The implications of this imagery are
yet to be realized.

Isaiah 50: 1-3

> 'Thus says the LORD: **Where is your mother's
> certificate of divorce, with which I sent her away**?
> Or which of my creditors is it to whom I have sold you?
> Behold, for your iniquities you were sold, and for your
> transgressions your mother was sent away. Why, when I
> came, was there no man; why, when I called, was there
> no one to answer? **Is my hand shortened, that it cannot
> redeem**? Or have I no power to deliver? Behold, **by my
> rebuke I dry up the sea, I make the rivers a
> desert;** their fish stink for lack of water and die of thirst.

> I clothe the heavens with blackness and make
> sackcloth their covering.'

The imagery of wife and child is now associated in a purposefully non literal manner. Israel, as a wife, has been divorced by God, and yet God is speaking to Israel as if she were the child of that same divorced wife. This carries a unique spiritual purpose.

While a child may be punished for its disobedience, it nevertheless always remains a child. This aspect portrays God's enduring promises irrespective of Israel's actions. On the other hand, a wife may be divorced for her unfaithfulness, and at that point she is no longer a wife. This aspect portrays God's total dissatisfaction with Israel and the permanent aspects of His judgment on those specific people at that time. But even God may eventually take back an unfaithful wife after divorce[67], which ironically was not permitted under the law.[68] We also note that this passage makes God both the father and husband of Israel, simultaneously.

God also integrates creation imagery into the passage, for the pattern must continue until we are overwhelmed by it. In this case, creation imagery is again portrayed in reverse, e.g. 'I dry up the sea, I make the rivers a desert…I clothe the heavens with blackness.'

Isaiah 51: 1-6

> 'Listen to me, you who pursue righteousness, you who
> seek the LORD: look to the rock from which you were
> hewn, and to the quarry from which you were dug. Look
> to Abraham your father and to Sarah who bore you;
> for he was but one when I called him, that I might bless
> him and multiply him. For the LORD comforts Zion;
> he comforts all her waste places and makes her
> wilderness like Eden, her desert like the garden of the
> LORD; joy and gladness will be found in her,
> thanksgiving and the voice of song. Give attention to
> me, my people, and give ear to me, my nation; for a
> law will go out from me, and I will set my justice for a
> light to the peoples. My righteousness draws near, my

---

[67] See also Jeremiah 3:1
[68] Deuteronomy 24:1-4

salvation has gone out, and my arms will judge the peoples; **the coastlands hope for me, and for my arm they wait. Lift up your eyes to the heavens, and look at the earth beneath; for the heavens vanish like smoke, the earth will wear out like a garment, and they who dwell in it will die in like manner**; but my salvation will be forever, and my righteousness will never be dismayed.'

Within the context of forward creation, God now intends to 'comfort Zion'. He will eventually alleviate the conditions of dry and dark, and 'comfort all her waste places and make her wilderness like Eden.' This wonderful transformation is commemorated with 'joy and gladness...thanksgiving, and the voice of song.' As evidence of this future promise, God invokes 'Abraham your father and...Sarah who bore you'. This correlation is very important, but will not be fully realized until we examine the NT.

The 'coastlands' are presented once more as an example of nonliteral creation imagery. They represent the 'peoples' who 'hope...and wait for me'. But what exactly are they waiting for? 'Lift up your eyes to the heavens', says Isaiah. 'The heavens vanish like smoke, the earth will wear out like a garment, and they who dwell in it will die.' Are we to think that this passage refers to the literal destruction of the creation of God? Certainly not, for the 'coastlands' themselves are part of that same creation.

But the 'coastlands' are waiting for the 'light', and according to the text that 'light' cannot come without first the destruction of the existing creation. This is, by definition, the role of reverse creation imagery. The 'former things' must first be destroyed, so to speak, that the 'new things' may be created. It is our task to understand this more fully within the context of the whole of Scripture.

Isaiah 51: 15-20

'I am the LORD your God, **who stirs up the sea so that its waves roar**-- the LORD of hosts is his name. And I have put my words in your mouth and covered you in the shadow of my hand, **establishing the heavens and laying the foundations of the earth, and saying to Zion, You are my people**. Wake yourself, wake

> yourself, **stand up, O Jerusalem, you who have drunk from the hand of the LORD the cup of his wrath**, who have drunk to the dregs the bowl, the cup of staggering. **There is none to guide her among all the sons she has borne; there is none to take her by the hand among all the sons she has brought up**. These two things have happened to you-- who will console you?-- devastation and destruction, famine and sword; who will comfort you? Your sons have fainted; they lie at the head of every street like an antelope in a net; they are full of the wrath of the LORD, the rebuke of your God.'

We noted above that mother Israel does have children, although she appeared to have forgotten about them for a time. Now Isaiah confirms for us that her children do exist, but at this point 'there are none to guide her'. She is a drunk and sleeping woman who is commanded to 'wake up'! This woman is also equivocated with the city itself, which is Jerusalem. All of this stands in parallel with our overarching theme. God has established 'the heavens and laid the foundations of the earth, and said to Zion, You are my people.' God's plans and God's creation are inseparable.

Isaiah 52: 1-3, 9-10

> '**Awake, awake, put on your strength, O Zion; put on your beautiful garments, O Jerusalem, the holy city**; for there shall no more come into you the uncircumcised and the unclean. **Shake yourself from the dust and arise; be seated, O Jerusalem**; loose the bonds from your neck, **O captive daughter of Zion**. For thus says the LORD: You were sold for nothing, and you shall be redeemed without money ... **Break forth together into singing, you waste places of Jerusalem, for the LORD has comforted his people; he has redeemed Jerusalem**. The LORD has bared his holy arm before the eyes of all the nations, and **all the ends of the earth shall see the salvation of our God**.'

'The holy city' of Jerusalem is instructed to awake and 'put on your beautiful garments', because as we have learned this city is also a woman. This is simply more evidence of the interchangeable nature of these specific non literal symbols.

Music also continues to play a role in the culmination of this imagery, and can be traced all the way back to the Song of Moses. 'Break forth together into singing...for the Lord has comforted His people...and *all* the ends of the earth shall see the salvation of our God.' The 'ends of the earth' are, of course, the 'coastlands' or 'nations' mentioned previously on several occasions.

Isaiah 54: 1-8

> **'Sing, O barren one, who did not bear; break forth into singing and cry aloud, you who have not been in labor! For the children of the desolate one will be more than the children of her who is married, says the LORD.** Enlarge the place of your tent, and let the curtains of your habitations be stretched out; do not hold back; lengthen your cords and strengthen your stakes. **For you will spread abroad to the right and to the left, and your offspring will possess the nations and will people the desolate cities.** Fear not, for you will not be ashamed; be not confounded, for you will not be disgraced; **for you will forget the shame of your youth, and the reproach of your widowhood you will remember no more. For your Maker is your husband, the LORD of hosts is his name**; and the Holy One of Israel is your Redeemer, the God of the whole earth he is called. **For the LORD has called you like a wife deserted and grieved in spirit, like a wife of youth when she is cast off, says your God. For a brief moment I deserted you, but with great compassion I will gather you.** In overflowing anger for a moment I hid my face from you, but with everlasting love I will have compassion on you, says the LORD, your Redeemer.'

The imagery of the woman Israel is particularly powerful in this passage. It is one of the most important for our understanding, and this is verified later in the NT.

At first glance, we observe that God appears to present Israel here as if she were two different women, i.e. the 'desolate one' and the 'married one' in v1. Both women ultimately have children, because the 'desolate one' has 'more'. But that is not the whole story. The 'desolate one' is 'like a wife deserted....like a wife of youth when she is cast off'. 'For a brief moment I deserted you, but with great compassion I will gather you'. The 'desolate one' was previously married to the *same* 'husband, the Lord of Hosts' who subsequently takes her back, e.g. 50:1-3.

This presents us with an interesting dilemma. Prior to the divorce of the 'desolate one', is God then married to both the 'married one' and the 'desolate one' at the same time? Or, alternatively, is there a way to reconcile these two women? There are several other places in the OT where God is presented as if He had two wives.[69] However, in each case, God's two wives are merely the two halves of the nation of Israel. And in each case *both* wives were temporarily divorced. But here throughout Isaiah we have no indication that God intends to represent the political and social divisions which arose between the northern and southern tribes. His purpose is to communicate His plan to include Gentiles in the promises made to the Jewish nation as a whole. This is utterly unaffected by the aforementioned interim Jewish divisions. Thus Israel has up to this point always been portrayed by Isaiah as a single woman, and will continue to be portrayed in that manner for the duration of the book. To insert such an abrupt break in the spiritual pattern, at this junction, would require extraordinary evidence.

It is critical then that we understand this within the context of the whole of Deutero-Isaiah. In reality, we find here two competing aspects of one woman's life, or Israel, presented in sequence. The 'desolate one' is really just the 'married one' who has been temporarily divorced and forgotten that she has children. The circumstances between the two aspects of the one woman are so different from one another that they are presented with the brief appearance of distinction. The former status of divorce will be 'remembered no more'. The new status of remarriage will cause Israel to 'sing....cry aloud'.

Once we acknowledge the possibility that there is only one woman under consideration here, another important point emerges. If the 'desolate one' is also the 'married one', then does that not mean that the 'desolate one' isn't really 'desolate'? Of course! Recall that

---

[69] Jeremiah 3, 31:31-32; Ezekiel 23

Israel had temporarily forgotten about her own symbolic children, e.g. 49:19-23, even though we know she had them to start, e.g. 51:18. So again, when Isaiah here refers to Israel as a 'barren one, who did not bear' it is *not* because she had no children up to this point. It is only because she did not 'bear' them.

The parallelism between 'bear' and 'labor' makes this clear. The pain of birth at the conclusion of the pregnancy is specifically under consideration in the imagery presented. We may understand then that Israel's 'children' are born without 'labor'. 'Who has borne me these...from where have these come'? God states that the 'desolate one' has 'not been in labor', which explains why she does not even realize she has children. When she is eventually remarried back to God, and her children are 'carried' back 'on the shoulders' of the 'nations', she will in fact have 'more' children. Isaiah will further reveal these other children as we progress.

The point is that there is no symbolic place for a second woman, without upending the context. Her position in the imagery would make no sense. The 'desolate' woman is simply unaware of the children she already has. To assign symbolic children to a second woman, who is apparently never divorced from God, clearly contradicts the imagery found later at the conclusion of Isaiah's prophecy. The symbolism of Jew and Gentile is fully encapsulated in one woman with many children.

Isaiah 60: 11-12, 14, 17-21

'Your gates shall be open continually; day and night they shall not be shut, that people may bring to you the wealth of the nations, with their kings led in procession. For the nation and kingdom that will not serve you shall perish; those nations shall be utterly laid waste. ... The sons of those who afflicted you shall come bending low to you, and all who despised you shall bow down at your feet; **they shall call you the City of the LORD, the Zion of the Holy One of Israel. ... Instead of bronze I will bring gold, and instead of iron I will bring silver; instead of wood, bronze, instead of stones, iron.** I will make your overseers peace and your taskmasters righteousness. Violence shall no more be heard in your land, devastation or destruction within your borders; **you**

> shall call your walls Salvation, and your gates Praise.
> The sun shall be no more your light by day, nor for
> brightness shall the moon give you light; but the
> LORD will be your everlasting light, and your God
> will be your glory. Your sun shall no more go down,
> nor your moon withdraw itself; for the LORD will be
> your everlasting light, and your days of mourning shall
> be ended. Your people shall all be righteous; they shall
> possess the land forever, the branch of my planting, the
> work of my hands, that I might be glorified.'

It is predicted that the Gentile nations will call Israel 'the city of the Lord'. Further, this city will be upgraded with new building materials. Specific materials with specific functions will each in turn be replaced with a superior material. Walls are constructed of 'salvation' and gates are constructed of 'peace'. The symbolic importance here is that some of the materials will be reused, i.e. 'bronze' and 'iron' but in a different capacity.

In parallel with the nonliteral building imagery, we have of course non literal creation imagery. The most important aspects of creation are represented as no longer necessary. 'The sun shall be no more your light by day, nor...the moon give you light.' God inserts Himself as 'your sun' and declares that He will 'no more go down.' Israel is then pictured as vegetation, or 'the branch of my planting, the work of my hands'. We should not continue to overlook the repetition of distinct imagery which, in the context of the spiritual mystery hidden from the beginning, is entirely interchangeable.

Isaiah 61: 8-11

> 'For I the LORD love justice; I hate robbery and
> wrong; I will faithfully give them their recompense, and
> I will make an everlasting covenant with them. Their
> offspring shall be known among the nations, and their
> descendants in the midst of the peoples; all who see
> them shall acknowledge them, that they are an offspring
> the LORD has blessed. I will greatly rejoice in the
> LORD; my soul shall exult in my God, for he has
> clothed me with the garments of salvation; he has
> covered me with the robe of righteousness, as a
> bridegroom decks himself like a priest with a beautiful
> headdress, and as a bride adorns herself with her

> jewels. **For as the earth brings forth its sprouts, and as a garden causes what is sown in it to sprout up**, so the Lord GOD will cause **righteousness and praise to sprout up before all the nations.**'

The symbolic woman and the symbolic city are clearly synonymous. The walls of the future city, which are made of 'salvation', are now translated into a 'garment'. This is the very same 'garment' for the woman that is referred to in 52:1-3, 9-10. Clothing is obviously intended for beauty, so that others may '*see the salvation of our God.*'

Similarly, the symbolic creation and the symbolic city are synonymous. The very same gates of the city, which are made of 'praise', are also the plant or 'people' of God which 'sprouts up' from the 'earth' 'before all the nations'.

Isaiah 62: 2-5; 11-12

> '**The nations shall see your righteousness**, and all the kings your glory, and **you shall be called by a new name that the mouth of the LORD will give.** You shall be a crown of beauty in the hand of the LORD, and a royal diadem in the hand of your God. You shall no more be termed Forsaken, and your land shall no more be termed Desolate, **but you shall be called My Delight Is in Her, and your land Married; for the LORD delights in you, and your land shall be married.** For as a young man marries a young woman, **so shall your sons marry you**, and as the bridegroom rejoices over the bride, so shall your God rejoice over you. ... **Behold, the LORD has proclaimed to the end of the earth**: Say to the daughter of Zion, Behold, your salvation comes; behold, his reward is with him, and his recompense before him. And they shall be called The Holy People, The Redeemed of the LORD; and you shall be called Sought Out, **A City Not Forsaken.**'

The stream of nonliteral imagery continues, as the prophet combines all of the symbols we have seen up to this point. The 'city not forsaken' is also defined to be the 'daughter of Zion' or 'the holy people'. So the woman and the city are interchangeable, as expected.

But there is more. Both the woman and the 'land' are married. Look closely at the Hebrew parallelism. In verse 4, we see three distinct phrases which place the woman in parallel with the land, and culminate with the marriage of both. But to whom is the land 'married'? As the NET Bible points out the land is 'married *to him*', that is God.[70] But so too is the woman married to God, all throughout Isaiah. So then the woman and the land are also interchangeable.

And there is even more. Verse 5 presents another staggering parallelism. 'As a young man marries a young woman, so shall *your sons* marry you.' Although this representation is completely foreign to us in the plain sense, it is the most accurate rendering of the text. Does the woman marry her own sons? Yes, but not in the sense that we might assume from our modern perspective. The original language is merely representing an important relationship between the woman and her sons.[71] This is not a physical, human marriage, any more than the marriage between the woman and God.

---

[70] 'That is, the land will be restored to the Lord's favor and once again enjoy his blessing and protection. To indicate the land's relationship to the Lord, **the words "to him" have been supplied at the end of the clause**.' Emphasis mine. See the NET Bible notes, Isaiah 62:4.

[71] The Hebrew text has 'your sons,' **but this produces an odd metaphor and is somewhat incongruous with the parallelism**. In the context (v. 4b, see also 54:5-7) **the Lord is the one who 'marries' Zion**. Therefore several prefer to emend 'your sons' to בֹּנָיִךְ (bonayikh, 'your builder'; e.g., NRSV). In Ps 147:2 the Lord is called the 'builder of Jerusalem.' **However, this emendation is not the best option for at least four reasons.** First, although the Lord is never called the 'builder' of Jerusalem in Isaiah, the idea of Zion's children possessing the land does occur (Isa 49:20; 54:3; cf. also 14:1; 60:21). Secondly, **all the ancient versions support the MT reading.** Thirdly, although the verb לְעָב (ba'al) can mean 'to marry,' its basic idea is 'to possess.' Consequently, **the verb stresses a relationship more than a state.** All the ancient versions render this verb 'to dwell in' or 'to dwell with.' **The point is not just that the land will be reinhabited, but that it will be in a relationship of 'belonging' to the Israelites.** Hence a relational verb like לְעָב is used (J. N. Oswalt, Isaiah [NICOT], 2:581). Finally, **'sons' is a well-known metaphor for 'inhabitants'** (J. de Waard, Isaiah, 208). Emphasis mine. See the NET Bible notes, Isaiah 62:5.

And who are the 'sons'? They are those who are 'carried' back on the 'shoulders' of the 'nations', e.g. 49:19-23.

So the woman and the land are one and the same, and they are married to the same person that is God. The woman is also married to her children. But the woman is also the city, which means the land and the city are one and the same as well. This is a marvelous correlation which we would not otherwise have been able to comprehend without considering Isaiah in its complete context. We have seen the most strange and unnatural imagery described throughout the book, which teaches us about the spiritual mystery hidden 'from the beginning'.

Isaiah 65: 16-19

> 'So that he who blesses himself in the land shall bless himself by the God of truth, and he who takes an oath in the land shall swear by the God of truth; because **the former troubles are forgotten and are hidden from my eyes. For behold, I create new heavens and a new earth, and the former things shall not be remembered or come into mind. But be glad and rejoice forever in that which I create; for behold, I create Jerusalem to be a joy, and her people to be a gladness. I will rejoice in Jerusalem and be glad** in my people; **no more shall be heard in it the sound of weeping** and the cry of distress.'

As we move closer to the climax of Isaiah's prophecy, God reminds Israel that the 'former troubles are forgotten and are hidden'. But these are not just any old 'former' troubles. These are specific, spiritual predictions made by God within the creation text that have come to pass, e.g. 42:1-9, 48:1-8. Now then God continues his theme of prediction via creation. He intends to 'create new heavens and a new earth', and by extension predict 'new' events, for the 'former things shall not be remembered nor come into mind'. 'They are created now, not long ago', as the prophet says in 48:7.

There is strong parallelism here which confirms our findings. God creates two things, and He states it two different ways. 'I create new heavens' stands in parallel with 'I create Jerusalem'. And again, 'a new earth' stands in parallel with 'her people'. Both the heavens and earth are part of the whole creation, and one cannot exist without the other. So too, as we have seen throughout Isaiah, the city itself is equated with the nation of Israel. Isaiah is simply teaching us about the interchangeable nature of the imagery of the 'new heavens and earth'. Of course, it was the destruction of the 'old' heavens and earth that was defined as punishment for Israel's rebellion.

Isaiah 66: 1-2; 7-14

'Thus says the LORD: **'Heaven is my throne, and the earth is my footstool; what is the house that you would build for me, and what is the place of my rest? All these things my hand has made, and so all these things came to be**, declares the LORD. But this is the one to whom I will look: he who is humble and contrite in spirit and trembles at my word... **Before she was in labor she gave birth; before her pain came upon her she delivered a son. Who has heard such a thing? Who has seen such things? Shall a land be born in one day? Shall a nation be brought forth in one moment? For as soon as Zion was in labor she brought forth her children. Shall I bring to the point of birth and not cause to bring forth?' says the LORD;** 'shall I, who cause to bring forth, shut the womb?' says your God.** 'Rejoice with Jerusalem, and be glad for her, all you who love her; rejoice with her in joy, all you who mourn over her; that you may nurse and be satisfied from her consoling breast; that you may drink deeply with delight from her glorious abundance.' For thus says the LORD: 'Behold, I will extend peace to her like a river, and the glory of the nations like an overflowing stream; and **you shall nurse, you shall be carried upon her hip, and bounced upon her knees. As one whom his mother comforts, so I will comfort you; you shall be comforted in Jerusalem**. You shall see, and your heart shall rejoice; your bones shall flourish like the grass; and the hand of the LORD shall be known to his servants, and he shall show his indignation against his enemies.'

All of creation is in fact the place of God's 'rest'. But this principle is not really true in a literal sense, for God is not a physical being at a point in space. 'Behold, heaven and the highest heaven cannot contain you.'[72] Within the context of Isaiah's creation commentary, therefore, Genesis 1 must continue to represent God's plan to bring together other nations of believers under the umbrella of the nation of Israel. This is the underlying spiritual theme which the heaven, as God's 'throne', and the earth, as God's 'footstool', conveys. Remember, the 'heaven' is also 'Jerusalem', and the 'earth' is also 'her people'. Everything must be placed in order, and all God's plans must eventually be fulfilled.

To make the point, Isaiah once more places the woman Israel and the creation side by side. '*Before* she was in labor she gave birth; *before* her pain came she delivered a son'. 'Who has heard' and 'who has seen'? Of all things most unnatural, this is exactly what we had already concluded about this 'barren' woman 'Zion'. Isaiah has told us that she would have 'more' children with God, once she was remarried to him, and now God has described the details of this new birth process. 'I bring to the point of birth,' says God through the prophet. So then all of Israel's children, both from the first marriage and the second, are born without physical pain. These children are adopted! This is precisely the imagery selected in the NT to represent God's plans to include Gentiles in Jewish promises,[73] which in turn verifies the lack of symbolic 'labor'. It is God, not Israel, who endures the actual labor process, both here and in 42:19.

So then we have confirmation that the two women apparently portrayed in 54:1-8 are actually one and the same. Jewish and Gentile believers are all included in the imagery of the one woman and her children. There is nothing left to be represented by a second woman, with distinct children. The other woman is merely the first stage of the one woman's life. She was married, and then divorced, and then remarried.

'Be glad for her, all you who love her'. Those who love the woman 'Zion' will 'nurse' and be 'carried upon her hip' and 'bounced upon her knees. They are her children, and these children will be comforted by their 'mother' which also happens to be the city of 'Jerusalem'.

---

[72] I Kings 8:27
[73] Romans 8:15, 23; 9:4; Galatians 4:5; Ephesians 1:5

Isaiah 66: 18-22

> 'For I know their works and their thoughts, and **the time
> is coming to gather all nations and tongues**. And they
> shall come and shall see my glory, and I will set a sign
> among them. And from them **I will send survivors to
> the nations**, to Tarshish, Pul, and Lud, who draw the
> bow, to Tubal and Javan, **to the coastlands far
> away, that have not heard my fame or seen my glory.
> And they shall declare my glory among the nations**.
> And they shall bring all your brothers from all the
> nations as an offering to the LORD, on horses and in
> chariots and in litters and on mules and on dromedaries,
> to my holy mountain Jerusalem, says the LORD, just as
> the Israelites bring their grain offering in a clean vessel
> to the house of the LORD. And some of them also I will
> take for priests and for Levites, says the LORD. '**For
> as the new heavens and the new earth that I make
> shall remain before me, says the LORD, so shall your
> offspring and your name remain**.'

'The time is coming to gather all nations and tongues'. Truly, we
could not summarize Isaiah's commentary on creation any better
than that. 'I will send survivors to the nations....to the *coastlands*
far away that have not heard my fame or seen my glory.' And
finally, 'they shall declare my glory among the nations'. With a
grand flourish, Isaiah confirms for us the eternal plans of God as
illustrated with the imagery of the heavens and earth. Recall the
specific parallelism found in 65:17-18, and compare with the
parallelism found here. The 'new heavens' are 'Jerusalem', and
now they are 'your offspring'. The 'new earth' is 'her people', and
now they are 'your name'. The 'offspring' in particular are the
nations of NT believers, both Jew and Gentile, symbolically born to
Israel without labor pain. That is, by adoption.

These images are all nonliteral in the sense that they are used. No
one would reasonably imagine otherwise, and that is precisely the
point. Literal cities cannot be built with praise and salvation, nor
can righteousness literally sprout out of the ground. God doesn't
have a literal wife, nor can women bear literal children without the
labor process. Women shouldn't marry their own literal children,
nor do they generally forget their own literal children. The literal
heavens don't vanish, nor do the literal seas dry up. The sun and

moon cannot literally be discarded, or else our planet would cease to function.

But let us reiterate the purpose of these interchangeable characters. Recall that Israel as the wife of God was briefly portrayed as two different women, for literary effect. Similarly, the city of God was portrayed in two different states. And yet, the two women are one and the same in the end. So too the new city is merely the old city, transformed with new and recycled materials. In precisely the same way, Genesis 1 rectifies an initial state of chaos and darkness, via process of forward creation. But it was God who first put the creation into that chaotic state. His judgments on Israel for their rebellion are explicitly described by Isaiah as creation, *in reverse*.

So then Isaiah's creation commentary explains to Israel how exactly Genesis 1 functions as a witness to God's covenant with all nations. It illustrates God's intent to undo the destruction that He has created, and replace it with salvation which He has also created. Isaiah reveals a 'new heaven and earth' for all nations, which immediately defines the previous 'heaven and earth' as 'old'. This 'old' creation was 'clothed with blackness', e.g. 50:3. It will 'vanish like smoke' and 'wear out like a garment', e.g. 51:6.

This is not a matter of one literal creation in Genesis 1, followed by a second symbolic creation abstracted from it in Deutero-Isaiah. Rather, the 'old' and the 'new' creations should be viewed as two phases of the same overall process, and they must go in sequence. This is the only way to maintain compatibility with the explicit pattern of the upgraded city and the remarried woman.

The prophet Jeremiah also supports this conclusion. He quotes the opening theme of Genesis 1, and places it explicitly in the **middle** of the covenant timeline of Deutero-Isaiah. [74] Right between the 'former' things of Israel's history, which culminate in the Assyro-Babylonian destruction, and the 'new' things in Israel's future, which culminate in God's promised covenant with all nations, lies the point of transition. Jeremiah says that this intermediate time period of captivity corresponds to the earth 'without form and void; and the heavens, they had no light.' He also says that this time

---

[74] Jeremiah 4:22-31

period is like 'the voice of a woman in travail, and the anguish as of her that bringeth forth her *first* child.'

But of course! Note that in 'former' times Isaiah says the Gentile nations who are represented by the 'coastlands' do 'hope' and 'wait' for salvation. God had intended to include them all along and so, even 'in the beginning' of Genesis 1, we see that water and a formless earth are represented under cover of darkness, just waiting for the new creation to begin.

This is the definitive OT witness to the spiritual mystery hidden 'from the beginning'. The references to God's plan for Gentile believers using interchangeable characters are so numerous and persistent in Isaiah's creation commentary, that the reader would make a serious mistake by overlooking their significance. No single symbol can account for all the different spiritual aspects that God desires to convey. We must have several different, interchangeable symbols to make clear the meaning of Genesis 1, and so we do.

VI.   The Allegory Of Creation

Genesis 1 is a model for the allegory genre in the NT. Paul recalls its imagery, by proxy, and expands upon it further. In doing so, he emphasizes deliberate contradictions with physical reality for a spiritual purpose.

Let us now discuss the particular literary technique utilized to construct the creation commentary of Deutero-Isaiah. Recall that the symbols of the woman, the city, and the creation are all deliberately applied in a non-literal fashion by the prophet, and also they are interchangeable. It is these specific characteristics which identify for us a form of literature that is all too often misused and abused. This is the allegory genre in the OT.

For many, the concept of allegory is obscure. It is accepted as legitimate, in theory, but in practice it is not well understood or defined. It would seem on the surface to be an elusive catch phrase for any type of spiritual symbolism we would like to superimpose upon any particular Biblical text. The fact is that alleged allegories are often arbitrary and speculative, and for no good reason. There exists an almost limitless number of ways in which one might claim allegorical meaning from any passage.

But it turns out there is only one explicit instance of the word 'allegory' in the whole Bible. In Galatians 4, Paul uses it to describe his spiritual exposition of Abraham's two wives and two sons. This certainly does not preclude the existence of other allegories elsewhere[75], but it does provide us with a clear test case for the genre.

---

[75] I Corinthians 10:1-11; Ephesians 5:22-33, etc.

Galatians 4:1, 3-5, 7, 22-31

'I mean that the heir, **as long as he is a child, is no different from a slave** though he is the owner of everything…In the same way we also, **when we were children, were enslaved to the elementary principles** of the world. But when the fullness of time had come, God sent forth his Son, born of woman, born under the law, to redeem those who were under the law, **so that we might receive adoption as sons…So you are no longer a slave, but a son**, and if a son, then an heir through God…For it is written that Abraham had two sons, one by a slave woman and one by a free woman. But the son of the slave was born according to the flesh, while the son of the free woman was born through promise. **Now this may be interpreted allegorically: these women are two covenants.** One is from Mount Sinai, bearing children for slavery; she is Hagar. **Now Hagar is Mount Sinai in Arabia; she corresponds to the present Jerusalem**, for she is in slavery with her children. **But the Jerusalem above is free, and she is our mother.** For it is written, '**Rejoice, O barren one who does not bear; break forth and cry aloud, you who are not in labor! For the children of the desolate one will be more than those of the one who has a husband.**' Now you, brothers, like Isaac, are children of promise. But just as at that time he who was born according to the flesh persecuted him who was born according to the Spirit, so also it is now. But what does the Scripture say? 'Cast out the slave woman and her son, for the son of the slave woman shall not inherit with the son of the free woman.' So, brothers, **we are not children of the slave but of the free woman.**'

Paul defines for us his allegory, based upon two women, and two cities. These symbols are drawn explicitly from Isaiah's commentary on creation, and Paul quotes the OT prophet so that the reader may be advised of this fact. He certainly follows the pattern of interchangeable characters, for example, found first in statements such as 'look to the rock from which you were hewn, and to the quarry from which you were dug. Look to Abraham your father and to Sarah who bore you'.[76] The parents of Isaac are directly

---

[76] Isaiah 51:1-2

compared with the creation, as if Israel were mined by God out of the ground like a precious metal. So Paul recognizes the spiritual parallels between the imagery of Isaiah and the circumstances of Sarah and Hagar.

But let us acknowledge that Sarah and Hagar do not explicitly come from Isaiah. Rather, the imagery of the woman Israel (in two parts) comes from Isaiah. Paul stands on Isaiah's shoulders, so to speak, and puts the pieces together. He contributes *additional* material to the imagery. This verifies that the basic technique, found first in the pages of Isaiah, is OT allegory.

Notice carefully what Paul does. He states, 'now this may be interpreted allegorically'. Literally, he is 'constructing an allegory based on the OT account.'[77] He takes a plain literal series of events, and draws a comparison between them and his intended spiritual message. And how exactly does he do that? Paul extracts themes from reality which communicate his point, and ignores those aspects of reality that contradict his point.

This is very surprising to consider at first. 'The natural person does not accept the things of the Spirit of God, for they are folly to him, and he is not able to understand them because they are spiritually discerned.'[78] We cannot presume then to understand the method of allegory without first observing this fundamental characteristic, as illustrated in the following table.

---

[77] See the NET Bible, Galatians 4:24
[78] I Corinthians 2:14

ALLEGORY	REALITY
Two Covenants	Two Women
Law, Liberty	Slave, Free
Flesh Persecutes Spirit	Older Persecutes Younger
ALLEGORY	**CONFLICT**
Bearing Children For Slavery	Ishmael Was Never A Slave
Barren Woman Is Divorced	Sarah Is Never Divorced
Barren Woman Has More Children	Sarah and Hagar Each Have One
Divorced Woman Is Remarried	Hagar Was Never Remarried
Children Born Without Labor Pain	Sarah and Hagar Experience Labor

Table 9: The Allegory Of Sarah And Hagar

While Paul's allegory is not derived out of thin air, nevertheless the real life story of Sarah and Hagar is *not* the allegory. The allegory of Sarah and Hagar is merely the comparison between their real life story and God's spiritual imagery, after the fact. It reflects the interchangeable, nonliteral characters of the spiritual mystery hidden 'from the beginning', and defined by Isaiah.

Paul confirms for us that these two symbolic women found first in the pages of Isaiah, are really one and the same. He observes that 'a child is no different from a slave', and goes on to say that 'when **we** were children, [we] were enslaved to the elementary principles of the world'. But 'you are **no longer** a slave, but a son!' And again, 'we are not children of the slave but of the free woman'. Although Sarah and Hagar were two different women, the symbolic 'children' only have one mother. First, the 'children' are slaves born to a slave woman. Then they transition and become free, born to a free woman. But these children are not born twice. The change in status for the children is merely dictated by the change in status of their mother. Paul emphatically states that 'Jerusalem **above** is free, and she is our mother'. This is taken directly from Isaiah 66:13, where the imagery of the city and the woman are equated. Of course, this city is 'above' because it is precisely the 'new heaven', which Isaiah also defines as 'Jerusalem'. And finally, this one woman or city is no longer a slave. She had been 'sold for her iniquities', as Isaiah says, or 'cast out' as Paul says. But Isaiah also tells us that she was 'redeemed without money' and subsequently remarried.

So then the allegory has a sound basis in past reality, but ultimately departs from it. Paul takes what makes sense, from past reality, and abandons what doesn't. He presumes explicit license to deviate from physical reality for the purpose of a spiritual point. Aspects from the story of Sarah and Hagar are selectively gleaned, and there is nothing wrong with this at all. The two women represent the stark contrast between the two stages of God's plan to include Gentiles in Jewish promises, although the overall plan itself was singular. The Gentiles were never intended to be second half substitutes.

> 'And there are what Paul, referring to Hagar and Sarah in Galatians 4:21-31, calls allegories. Notably, I Corinthians 9:8-10 states explicitly that in Deuteronomy 25:4 Moses was speaking for *our* (Christians') sake. The precise way in which the Corinthians passage ought to be interpreted may be disputed, but it is one of several that help us conclude that for Paul, as for several other authors under review in this study, **the literal sense is subordinated to an allusive or allegorical sense, even if the literal is not rejected.** ...
>
> To Paul-the first Christian interpreter of the OT-the Scriptures speak of, anticipate, typologize, *reveal* Christ and him crucified. In effect, Paul takes the spectrum of Jewish hermeneutical methods-literal, allegorical, midrashic-and uses these instruments in a completely new way. In so doing, he says things that are revolutionary to the Jews **but in a language and framework very much their own.**'[79]

---

[79] Peter Bouteneff, *Beginnings: Ancient Christian Readings of the Biblical Creation Narratives*, (Baker Academic, Grand Rapids MI, 2008), 39.

It is clear that Paul's perspective represents a paradigm shift. He is working very hard to make his audience think deeply, in ways they have never thought before. But not once does Paul ever imply that his audience should mentally pivot in a new spiritual direction on his authority alone, as a novel expositor. Not once. On the contrary, Paul quotes Isaiah time and again to make his point. Paul and Isaiah are both creating allegories, using the same type of imagery, for the same overall purpose. So Paul insists that he is only the vessel to rebroadcast the spiritual pivot which has *already* occurred. In reality, Isaiah's creation commentary reveals the spiritual pivot. That is, a pivot to the Gentiles.

This realization has broad implications for the text of Genesis 1. Creation is the 'beginning' of the story, says Isaiah, and our job is to recognize what *he* says that story is. 'I was ready to be sought **by those who did not ask for me**; I was ready to be found **by those who did not seek me**... For behold, **I create new heavens and a new earth**, and the former things shall not be remembered or come into mind. **But be glad and rejoice forever in that which I create**. For behold, I create Jerusalem to be a joy, and her people to be a gladness.'[80] The story is of Israel, and all nations, from birth to salvation. That is the literal, historical basis in past reality, from which the allegory is drawn. That is the source to which the imagery of the woman, the city, and the creation point. But God did not wait to choose the Gentiles, until after His people Israel did not meet His expectations. The point of all this is that the spiritual pivot doesn't occur in Paul's text, and it doesn't occur in Isaiah's either. God was actually 'ready' for the Gentiles 'from the beginning.

God was so 'ready' for the Gentiles, in fact, that He proposed to completely destroy His 'creation' so that it would not even 'come into mind.' He would replace it with a 'new creation' entirely. 'Let them bring their witnesses to prove them right, and let them hear and say, It is true. 'You are my witnesses,' declares the LORD.'[81] Israel's function as a witness does no good if there was no one else

---

Emphasis mine.

[80] Isaiah 65:1, 17-18
[81] Isaiah 43:9, 10

around to receive that witness. Enter the Gentiles, stage right.
'Bring my sons from afar and my daughters from the end of the
earth, everyone who is called by my name, **whom I created for my
glory, whom I formed and made**....All the nations gather together,
and the peoples assemble.'[82]

Irrespective of the fact that God's plan for the Gentiles was not
actually *explained* 'from the beginning', nevertheless it must have
existed 'from the beginning'. Why else would God have created all
other nations in the first place? So the fact is that where Paul points
back to Isaiah, using allegory, Isaiah then points back to creation,
using allegory. The goal for both authors is simply to convince
Israel of these things via common sense observations and dramatic
imagery.

But why do the allegories of Isaiah and Paul require a deliberate
retelling of past historical reality to make the point? The answer,
perhaps, may become obvious with some thought. The fact is that
any real life human story, when examined in detail, will become
woefully inadequate on its own to convey God's spiritual message.
There will inevitably be some contradictions between physical
reality, and God's perfect spiritual plan. The lives of Sarah and
Hagar are merely a case in point.

Therefore allegorical contradictions with reality do not undermine
the real life story. At the same time, an allegory is only a rough
approximation of historical reality. This is not a philosophical trick.
It is only to accept the use case for allegory that Scripture actually
defines. Allegories are constructed from reality, and they are the
complete opposite of arbitrary. They are literally a compromise
between the physical reality, and the spiritual reality. We as NT
participants in God's covenant unfortunately often blur the two, so
that we do not recognize the difference.

And Isaiah's 'new creation' should help revive this critical
distinction. This 'new heaven and earth', which is also an upgraded
city 'above' and a remarried 'mother', must replace the old creation.
So these allegorical symbols all have two phases. Two, spiritual
phases. This explains why neither Isaiah nor Paul 'allegorize' the

---

[82] Isaiah 43:6, 7, 9

literal details of Genesis 1, and assign 'new' meaning to them after the fact. That would imply that a spiritual creation could replace a physical creation, which makes no sense. Instead Isaiah, and Paul by proxy, require that the text lie untouched, exactly as written, because it is *already* compiled properly to make the 'new' point. Genesis 1 is called to mind by Isaiah over and over, with the use of the word אָרָב (bara')[83], to show Israel that whatever their opinion of the text so far, they had not yet comprehended its spiritual meaning with respect to the Gentiles. For example, Genesis 1 explicitly opens with existing material in ruins, and Isaiah explains to the Jews in captivity why this intermediate state of destruction exists via creation in reverse.[84]

There is obviously no physical evidence that the literal creation was ever destroyed and remade by God in this fashion. And it doesn't make any sense to insist that it must have been so either. We cannot expect to reverse engineer the historical details of the past from spiritual allegory. It is therefore reasonable to accept that Isaiah and Paul are just using a literary genre which intentionally deviates from physical reality to make a spiritual point. God's 'new heaven' and 'new earth' are replacements.

---

[83] See also CH1 – The Mystery Of Creation
[84] See also CH5 – The Symbols Of Creation

VII. The Dilemma of Creation

Genesis 1 intentionally differs from several other creation stories in the Bible, as a result of its unique, spiritual task.

The accounts of creation in the Bible present us with a controversy of such scale that the pages of Genesis cannot contain it. Dr. Jeffrey Tigay summarizes this important, and yet often ignored, issue succinctly.

> '[There are] several accounts of creation in the Bible even though no two accounts agree in detail with Genesis 1 or with each other. ... [These] are found in poetic form in Psalms, Proverbs, and Job. ... Genesis 1 speaks of the prehistoric waters in purely naturalistic terms and says that God merely commanded that they gather in a single spot so that dry land could appear. But in the poetic passages the ancient waters are personified as rebellious sea-monsters which threatened to swamp the dry land, until God subdued them and created the seashore as a boundary which they were prohibited from crossing. The most notable difference between Genesis and all the other accounts is that none of the others mentions the idea that the world was created in six days. This idea ...was apparently not considered important enough in the Bible to be repeated in other accounts of creation.
>
> The fact that so many differing accounts were all accepted in the Bible shows that its compilers were not concerned about these details. They undoubtedly assumed that the differences could be reconciled, but they left this task to the ingenuity of exegetes. This virtually assured that different reconciliations would be proposed and that some of the passages would have to be interpreted non-literally.'[85]

---

[85] Jeffrey Tigay, 'Genesis, Science, and 'Scientific Creationism' ', 1988,

It is intriguing that, in certain circles, so little discussion is had regarding the inconsistencies between texts alluded to above. Indeed, however the reader desires to read Genesis 1, they nevertheless are tasked with the extra burden of reconciling all of the other, parallel creation stories to it. The impact of this realization is significant, as Dr. Tigay infers, in that the OT text does not explicitly reconcile this for us. The apparent conflict is left as an open ended question.

Dr. Mark Smith has also written extensively in an effort to promote a deeper understanding of these various creation accounts throughout the OT. He states, 'In ancient Israel, people told the creation story in different ways, as we see in various biblical books. There are allusions to the creation story in the prophets (for example, Jer. 10:12; Amos 4:13, 9:6; Zech. 12:1), and it is recounted in various wisdom books (Prov. 8:22-31; Job 26:7-13, 38:1-11; Ben Sira 1:3-4, 24:3-9). The creation story was also a topic in Israel's worship (Pss. 74:12-17, 89:11-13, 90:2, and 148). These passages show us that in ancient Israel many different creation accounts existed, not just one single creation story. In fact, these passages indicated that there were various ways of telling the creation story. ... Various creation accounts present God as a warrior-king, as a wise ruler, or as the great monarchic presence in his palace or builder of his sanctuary space. All of these were old ideas in the ancient world well before the historical emergence of Israel.'[86]

Dr. Peter Bouteneff explains, 'The Hexaemeron [six day] account is unapologetically followed by a paradise narrative that recounts creation in a different sequence and ... allusions to creation in the Psalms, Job, and Isaiah vary from it and from each other.'[87] So then, in the face of all this, a single point begins to emerge. The various Biblical creation accounts together begin to foster doubt as to which of them, if any, should represent *the* authoritative, literal version of creation. If God was so intent on ensuring that His followers knew and understood the *precise,* literal mechanics of His

---

<http://www.sas.upenn.edu/~jtigay/sci.htm> (15 Dec 2014).
[86] Mark Smith, *The Priestly Vision of Genesis 1*, (Fortress Press, 2010), 11-12.
[87] Peter Bouteneff, *Beginnings: Ancient Christian Readings of the Biblical Creation Narratives*, (Baker Academic, Grand Rapids MI, 2008), 2.

creative process, then why would He permit such confusion? While the reader may suggest that all of these creation variants are quite complementary, rather than conflicting, this suggestion is simply unsustainable. The diversity of creation texts in the Bible cannot be equivocated with the wave of a magic wand. They are significantly different. The most honest response is not to deny this plain fact, but rather to determine why it is so.

In particular, the dueling creation accounts of Genesis play a significant role in this investigation. There are several blatant conflicts between Genesis 1 and 2 if both texts are read plainly, and in parallel, as the following table illustrates.[88]

Genesis 1-2:4a	Genesis 2:4b-3:24
Creation is divided into days.	No days or other periods of time are mentioned.
Creation has a cosmic scope.	Creation has to do with the earth only.
Animals are created before man.	Man created before animals.
Animals are part of a cosmic design (along with plants and everything else)	Animals are created for a limited purpose: to keep man company or be "a helper"-- though they turn out to be unsuitable for Adam, forcing God to make Eve instead.
Man is to rule the world.	Man is to have charge of Eden only and, presumably, is never to leave it.
Woman is created simultaneously with man.	Woman is created after (and from) the body of man.

Only the deity speaks.	Four speakers engage in dialogue, one of them an animal.
The fruit of every tree is given for food.	The deity forbids eating the fruit of a tree.
Man and woman have dominion over all living creatures, including those in the sea.	Man does not interact with living creatures of the sea, nor does he name them.
All the water over the surface of the entire earth is gathered into one place.	A river flows out of Eden and divides into four.

Table 10: Creation Conflicts In Genesis

An overwhelming amount of historical effort has been put forth, in an attempt to overcome these creation difficulties. But our primary purpose here is not to examine those attempts in detail. The author will merely observe in a general sense that such efforts are revealing. They prove that the individual, who insists on inter-textual agreement would do or say anything to save them as a single, cohesive, literal description of the physical creation. Their pious efforts, while noble at heart, ironically ignore the plain reading, in an effort to save their various interpretations of the plain reading which themselves are not so plain. But we cannot jump through hoops, while at the same time asserting simplicity and consensus of interpretation.

Wide ranging attempts to harmonize the creation texts of Genesis not only prove the difficulty of the task at hand, but also verify the legitimacy of the conflicts raised. The supposedly plain words on the page are anything but. They prove that serious work must be

---

[88] The majority of this table was taken from John Gabel et al, *The Bible As Literature*, (Oxford University Press, 2005) 90. Additional important conflicts have been added for reference by the author.

done by the interpreter. Simply taping the texts together, and painting over the differences, does not do justice in the least to a conundrum that God has purposefully presented to us for review. So then we should expect to find evidence of this conflict throughout history, and so we do.

But these conflicts are not forced upon the text by unbelievers and skeptics who despise God or deny His existence. The object here is not to devalue Scripture. Far from it, the object here is to honor Scripture and seek to understand it as it stands without modification. It would certainly be easier, and much preferred, if these conflicts did not exist. But they do, whether we choose to ignore them or not.

For example, one point put forth in favor of a chronological overlap between Genesis 1 and 2 is that Jesus himself refers to the male and female from both creation texts in sequence. [89] But this is not as straightforward as it might appear. In the first place, the presumed correspondence between the creation texts has presented many challenges to interpretation throughout history. In the second place, the teaching of Christ on marriage and divorce makes much more spiritual sense if the two texts are not forcibly merged.[90]

Another popular method of reconciling the Genesis texts is the unique translation of a key phrase found in Genesis 2:19. [91] But this method is untenable; it simply creates more problems. If such an approach was viable the Jews themselves, as the preeminent experts

---

[89] Matthew 19:3-12
[90] See Appendix V. He Created Them Male And Female
[91] 'To harmonize the order of events with the chronology of chapter one, some translate the prefixed verb form with *vav* (ו) consecutive as a past perfect ("had formed," cf. NIV) here [Gen 2:19]. (In chapter one the creation of the animals preceded the creation of man; here the animals are created after the man.) However, **it is unlikely that the Hebrew construction can be translated in this way in the middle of this pericope, for the criteria for unmarked temporal overlay are not present here**. See S. R. Driver, *A Treatise on the Use of the Tenses in Hebrew*, 84-88, and especially R. Buth, "Methodological Collision between Source Criticism and Discourse Analysis," *Biblical Hebrew and Discourse Linguistics*, 138-54. For a contrary viewpoint see *IBHS* 552-53 §33.2.3 and C. J. Collins, "The *Wayyiqtol* as 'Pluperfect': When and Why," *TynBul* 46 (1995): 117-40.' See the NET Bible notes, Gen. 2:19. Emphasis mine.

in their own language, would not have otherwise bothered to waste their time. They could very easily have made this type of textual correction, if it was feasible, but they did not. The fact is that there are no ancient witnesses which support such a modification of Scripture. The overwhelming majority of modern linguistic scholars also agree on this point.[92, 93]

Fred Clark summarizes the issue this way.

> 'That the Bible does, indeed, contain very different versions of various stories is fairly obvious if you pick it up and start reading at the beginning of either of the testaments. Matthew's Gospel begins with a genealogy and a nativity story. So does Luke's Gospel. But they are not the *same* genealogy and nativity story. Genesis starts with a creation story. And then it follows that with a *different* creation story.
>
> Right off the bat, then, we have a choice to make. We can choose to accept that this apparent variation is a feature of the book(s) we are reading, and we can then go about trying to learn what such variation has to teach us. Or we can choose to say that this appearance of variation is a problem that must be solved, and we can then go about trying to explain away every such apparent instance of variety, dispute or diversity within the canon.'[94]

So what then does this variation between creation accounts have to teach us about Genesis 1?

---

[92] Wikipedia contributors. "Genesis creation narrative." *Wikipedia, The Free Encyclopedia*. Wikipedia, The Free Encyclopedia, 20 May. 2015. Web. 21 May. 2015.
[93] L. Kip Wheeler, 'What Are the J, E, and P Texts of Genesis', 2014, <https://web.cn.edu/kwheeler/Genesis_texts.html> (21 May 2015).
[94] Fred Clark, 'Fanon and Canon: 'Harmonizing' away the Bible', 6 Aug 2013, < http://www.patheos.com/blogs/slacktivist/2013/08/06/fanon-and-canon-harmonizing-away-the-bible/> (26 Jan 2015).

UNIQUE	An introduction stands apart from the main body of text, with unique structure and form.
PURPOSE	An introduction accomplishes a specific purpose, which the main body of text alone cannot accomplish.
TRANSITION	An introduction bridges the divide between itself and the main body of text.

Table 11: Framework Of A Literary Introduction

First, as Dr. John Walton notes, 'The book clearly has one outstanding compositional feature: it is organized around eleven sections with each governed by a toledot formula. The first of these formulas comes in 2:4: 'This is the account (toledot) of the heavens and earth when they were created.' The other ten are connected to individuals (Adam, Noah, Shem, etc.).'[95] The toledot structure naturally forms a chronological sequence throughout Genesis.

However, Genesis 1 is conspicuously *not* defined to be a toledot (account) at all. It is a distinctly different type of narrative than that which is found throughout the remainder of Genesis.[96] The

---

[95] Andrew Hill and John Walton, *A Survey of The Old Testament*, (Zondervan Publishing House, 1991) 91-92.

[96] 'The literary genre of Genesis 1 may be classified broadly as prose narrative. (Even the label narrative is potentially misleading, though, since Genesis 1 has no plot and no character development.) **It is not written in Hebrew poetry, since it lacks parallelism, but it is not composed in typical Hebrew prose, either**. Its syntax or sentence construction is different in degree if not in kind from what we find in normal narrative prose. It is marked by formulaic repetitions, tight symmetries, and an elevated style. **There is nothing quite like it anywhere in the Hebrew Bible**, certainly not among Old Testament historical narratives. In its literary compactness, exalted tone and solemn contents, it most resembles passages such as Psalm 104, Job 38, and Proverbs 8—all of which are in Hebrew poetry.' Emphasis mine. See Daniel Harlow, 'Creation According to Genesis: Literary Genre, Cultural Context, Theological

common misconception that Genesis 2 simply stands as a detailed review of certain previous events in Genesis 1 is strained and has led many expositors down a difficult path. The original language instead vividly reveals a much more complex circumstance. [97]

The OT scholar Dr. Gordon Wenham agrees.

> 'Chapter 1 is a carefully constructed unit in its own right, which equips the reader with the theological spectacles that enables him to read the subsequent material with the correct focus. **There are various marks of careful editing** that characterize chapter 1... Both 1:1-2 and 2:1-3 are multiples of seven words: 1:1 consists of seven words, 1:2 of fourteen (7x2), and 2:1-3 of thirty-five (7x5) words. Other key terms in 1:1 – 2:3 are also multiples of seven: God occurs thirty-five times, earth twenty-one times, and the clauses 'and it was so' and 'God saw that it was good' also occur seven times. This preference for multiples of seven draws attention to the

---

Truth' *Christian Scholar's Review* 37 (2008): 170.
<https://www.calvin.edu/academic/religion/faculty/harlow/Creation%20ac cording%20to%20Genesis.pdf>
[97] 'The Hebrew phrase תֹדְלֹות הָלֵא ('elle tolẏdot) is traditionally translated as "these are the generations of" because the noun was derived from the verb "beget." Its usage, however, shows that it introduces more than genealogies; **it begins a narrative that traces what became of the entity or individual mentioned in the heading**. In fact, a good paraphrase of this heading would be: "This is what became of the heavens and the earth," for **what follows is not another account of creation** but a tracing of events from creation through the fall and judgment (the section extends from 2:4 through 4:26). See M. H. Woudstra, "The Toledot of the Book of Genesis and Their Redemptive-Historical Significance," CTJ 5 (1970): 184-89. ... Although some would make the heading in 2:4 a summary of creation (1:1–2:3), **that goes against the usage in the book**. As a heading it introduces the theme of **the next section**, the particulars about this creation that God made. **Genesis 2 is not a simple parallel account of creation**; rather, beginning with the account of the creation of man and women, the narrative tells what became of that creation. As a beginning, the construction of 2:4-7 forms a fine parallel to the construction of 1:1-3. The subject matter of each תֹדְלֹות (tolẏdot, "this is the account of") section of the book **traces a decline or a deterioration through to the next beginning point, and each is thereby a microcosm of the book which begins with divine blessing in the garden, and ends with a coffin in Egypt.**' See the NET Bible notes, Genesis 2:4. Emphasis mine.

seventh day, the Sabbath, the day when God rested from
His acts of creation. …

> **This careful structuring of this first account of
> creation sets it apart from the material** that follows in
> the subsequent chapters. **So does the language.**
> Whereas 2:4 onwards is straightforward Hebrew
> narrative prose, 1:1 – 2:3 has a poetic flavor, and though
> some scholars have termed it poetry **it is better
> described as elevated prose. It certainly has a
> different character** from the later chapters of Genesis.'[98]

Second, Isaiah and Paul make it quite plain that God did predict
future events, in spiritual terms, 'from the beginning'. This timeline
of events necessarily focuses on Christ, and the nations of NT
believers, both Jew and Gentile. Genesis 1 must somehow therefore
represent these future events in a way in which no single toledot in
the following sequence could do. It must necessarily supersede the
toledot sequence which ends, as noted by the NET Bible, in ruins!
Thus Genesis 1 functions with a distinctly different purpose.

Dr. Wenham continues,

> 'But can one be more specific about its genre? Hermann
> Gunkel called it 'faded myth' while Von Rad said it was
> not myth or saga but priestly doctrine. There is some
> merit in both these descriptions, but better than both is
> Westermann's description of this section **as an overture.**
> An overture opens an opera and introduces some of the
> key themes and tunes that **will be developed later: this
> is what Gen 1 does for the rest of the book.** In Gen 1
> we meet for the first time some of the chief actors and
> learn something about their character. … The goal of
> creation is that God should 'rest,' i.e., dwell with man.
> **All students of Scripture will recognize theological
> motifs in Gen 1 that are developed more fully later in
> Genesis, indeed in the rest of the Bible.**'[99]

Third, the transition between Genesis 1 and the main body of the
toledot sequence is a literary seam, framed in very unique terms. It

---

[98] Charles Halton et al, *Genesis: History, Fiction, or Neither?*, (Zondervan,
2015), 79-80. Emphasis mine.
[99] Halton et al, *Genesis*, 80. Emphasis mine.

does not match the pattern subsequently employed between the eleven toledot of Genesis. 'There is chiastic linkage between the opening verse (1:1) and the closing verses (2:1-3). Verse 1 literally reads 'In the beginning *created* (A), *God* (B), *heavens and earth* (C)' and **these terms reappear in reverse order** in 2:1-3.'[100] This reversal is enlightening. In a phrase, it perfectly illustrates God's future purpose with His creation. That is to say that the Divine perspective, first from heaven to earth, is intended to be reversed. God desires our focused response back to Him, as a result of our creation, from earth to heaven.[101]

In other words, the literary transition from Genesis 1 to the following toledot sequence identifies a relationship that is complementary rather than equivalent. It is an obvious bridge, constructed for us within the text so that we might follow it where it leads.

> 'The key in interpreting the Bible is not my applying a personal philosophical or hermeneutical grid over the text but allowing the intent of the inspired original authors to fully express themselves. **To take a literary passage and demand it to be literal when the text itself gives clues to its symbolic and figurative nature imposes my biases on a divine message. Genre (type of literature) is the key in a theological understanding** of 'how it all began' and 'how it will all end.' … Parts of the Bible are surely historical narrative. There is a place for the literal interpretation of Scripture: there was a call of Abraham, an Exodus, a virgin birth, a Calvary, a resurrection; there will be a second coming and an eternal kingdom. **The question is one of genre, not reality, of authorial intent, not personal preferences** in interpretation. Let all men be liars--and God be true (cf. Rom. 3:4)!'[102]

---

[100] Halton et al, *Genesis*, 79. Emphasis mine.

[101] In his discussion of the **change in viewpoint** from God the Creator in Genesis 1 to humanity in 2:4b and following, Nahum Sarna similarly observes: 'This shift in perspective and emphasis is signaled by the inversion of the regular sequence 'heaven and earth' in the opening sentence.' Emphasis mine. See Smith, 'Priestly Vision'.

[102] Robert Utley, *How It All Began: Genesis 1-11*, (Bible Lessons International, 2013). Emphasis mine. <http://www.freebiblecommentary.org/old_testament_studies/VOL01AOT

The impact of these three general observations[103] cannot be overstated. Together, they demonstrate how Genesis 1 is actually an introduction to the remainder of the book. Additional literary and textual analysis also supports this conclusion[104], and we must further acknowledge the implications of this definition. It is only

---

/VOL01AOT_01.html>

[103] 'The juxtaposition of Gen 1 to the Eden narrative demands that they be read in light of each other. When done so, **three considerations emerge**. First, there are discrepancies between the two accounts. Most notable are the discrepancies in 'chronology'. ... The two accounts exhibit different foci. Gen 1 maintains its focus on the earth in a universal sense. Although the focus of the Eden narrative may have begun with the universal in 2:4-7, it is quickly honed to a focus on the garden. ... Second, the discrepancies are indicative that the two creation accounts serve different functions. As Sternberg notes concerning the structure of repetition, '**any discrepancies within a series of members that apparently issue from the narrator himself reflect changes not in his powers and circumstances but in his choices and goals.**' ... Third, two points emerge from Gen 2:4: (1) Gen 2:4 possesses a **retrospective** function and (2) the *toledot* formula a **prospective** function as a heading to the narrative it precedes.' Emphasis mine. See Ben Davis, 'Genesis 1:1-2:3 As A Theological Blueprint', 2014, < https://www.academia.edu/6675210/GENESIS_1_1-2_3_AS_A_THEOLOGICAL_BLUEPRINT_FOR_GOD_S_CREATION AL_ABODE_A_PROPOSAL> (Nov 2015).

[104] 'Genesis 1...may serve as the priestly **prologue** to what follows in Genesis and as a sort of implicit 'priestly' **commentary** on the so called 'second' creation account. ... Critics have long noted the dense and deliberate character of this text, which reflects its role as an introduction. ... **The specific frame of reference for the narrow commentary of Genesis 1:1-2:4a is Genesis 2:4b and following**... There is a particular verbal affinity between Genesis 1:1 and 2:4b. Ephraim Speiser in noting the connection states: 'the difference is by no means accidental.' Claus Westermann thinks that, 'since v 4b clearly refers to Gen1 and is similar to the introduction, 1:1, it can be understood as a prefix which makes it easier to join Gen 2-3 to Gen 1.' Westermann then cites a statement of Werner Schmidt: 'It forms a transition from the priestly to the Yahwistic story of creation.' Emphasis mine. See Mark Smith, *The Priestly Vision of Genesis 1*, (Fortress Press, 2010), 118, 128-130. He also discusses several other grammatical parallels between Genesis 1 and Genesis 2 that support this same premise.

from the Biblical perspective of Isaiah and Paul that we may more fully realize the extent to which the text works as an introduction.

Thus the aforementioned discontinuities between creation accounts in the Bible should not come as a surprise, but rather are to be expected. We cannot simply ignore the wide variety of ancient creation accounts contained within the OT, including Genesis 2, which only exaggerate the fact that the plain literal events of Genesis 1 are not so plain. These conflicts represent a critical, literary marker, by which we may more easily identify the spiritual purpose of Genesis 1.

The attentive reader may now perceive a discrepancy. Does the first toledot stand as a 'second' creation account, per our initial sources, or is it rather 'not another account of creation'? These two positions appear to be mutually exclusive. On the one hand, the author reaffirms that there are several blatant conflicts between Genesis 1 and 2:4-4:26 if both texts are read plainly, and in parallel. This, by definition, requires that they are 'different', and these differences have always been observed historically. There is absolutely nothing the reader can do to reverse this conflict in the plain reading, as if they were a linguistic magician. In that sense, the first toledot is indeed a 'second' account of creation.

On the other hand, the literary evidence discussed strongly indicates that Genesis 1 is a Divine introduction to the story of the heaven and earth, written for a different purpose using very different terms. While the toledot sequence is told from the perspective of man, Genesis 1 is quite the opposite. God's perspective of His future plans for His universe incorporates the end from the beginning. That is to say, again, we know that God intended to convey His spiritual plans in this specific text. It should come as no surprise, therefore, that the perspectives of God and man would be inherently different. Genesis 1 stands out from the backdrop of the toledot sequence like a neon sign.

In that sense, the first toledot is not a 'second' account of creation, any more than an apple can be a second orange. We must acknowledge the introductory framework, so that we might understand its effect upon our modern interpretation of Genesis 1. God has provided a great wealth of information elsewhere in the Bible which explains His Divine, spiritual intent 'in the beginning'.

Yet at the same time, He has not provided any explicit commentary on the plain literal meaning of Genesis 1 for the modern audience, or on the plain literal discrepancies between Genesis 1 and all other Biblical creation accounts. All attempts to reconcile the text of Genesis 1 with other creation texts have thus seemed to miss the point. No other Biblical creation passage is remotely capable of performing the particular, spiritual task that is assigned to it by Isaiah and Paul. So then it is much more reasonable to accept the fact that this spiritual task requires the text to be intentionally different.

VIII. The Conclusion Of Creation

The creation of our world, as revealed in Genesis 1, is a spiritual mystery that conveys a non-literal sense. It is associated with parables, time and again throughout scripture. And the creative sequence was explained to Israel by the prophet Isaiah. His imagery helps make sense of the deliberate contradictions between Genesis 1, and other Biblical creation texts. Therefore, it is reasonable to conclude that Genesis 1 is itself an allegory, or OT parable.

Some believers would defend the notion that Genesis 1 is a rigid, mechanical description of specific past events in the modern sense. They would demand that any view to the contrary be condemned as a sign of spiritual weakness, and assert that their fellow believers who do not agree do not have sufficient faith in the plain literal text. But those who are so intent on defending this literal text cannot hope to achieve anything but perpetual debate.

> 'Christianity has been forced to be content with a number of alternatives on the table for interpreting the early chapters of Genesis. It is sadly true that some have adopted a view that only their particular parochial reading is legitimate for a 'real' Christian. We must confess to our corporate shame that blood has even been spilled.
>
> As interpreters of Scripture and as theologians, we are accountable to the Biblical text. As important as our theological traditions are, since interpretations and even the hermeneutics by which we interpret have changed over the centuries, we cannot be unflinchingly accountable to tradition at every level. Several hundred

years ago renewed access to the original languages had significant impact on Biblical interpretation. In recent decades, the availability of documents from the ancient world has provided a remarkable resource for our reading of the Biblical text. We dare not neglect these tools when they can contribute so significantly to our interpretation.'[105]

The assumption of a modern perspective on Genesis 1 turns out to be flawed, and the conclusion of this work is, ironically, simple. Genesis 1 is itself, most likely, an allegory, or OT parable. Spiritual weakness is not defined by a lack of commitment to the literal text, but rather by an inability to account for *how* the spiritual meaning of that text, defined elsewhere in the Bible, actually affects that literal text. Until we have comprehended this more substantial meaning, we are not really in any position at all to defend any one of the many different literal readings which have been proposed over the centuries, with respect to the creation of our physical world.

Let us revisit our seven spiritual principles of Genesis 1.

MYSTERY	Genesis 1 contains a hidden, spiritual mystery.
SONG	Genesis 1 conveys a nonliteral sense.
PARABLES	Genesis 1 is associated with parables.
SABBATH	Genesis 1 is a specific, spiritual sequence of days.
SYMBOLS	Genesis 1 is explained with interchangeable characters.
ALLEGORY	Genesis 1 is the model for the allegory genre in the NT.
DILEMMA	Genesis 1 intentionally differs from other creation texts.

Table 12: Seven Principles Revisited

---

[105] John Walton, *The Lost World of Adam and Eve*, (InterVarsity Press, 2015), 2- 3.

The enigma of creation is thus a challenge which encourages us to think deeply. This challenge is purposeful, and of Divine origin. We cannot ignore these spiritual principles established by Isaiah and Paul. Who are we to define God's version of truth for Him? Was it not His decision to reveal His own creation text in just this way? 'But who are you, O man, to answer back to God? Will what is molded say to its molder, 'Why have you made me like this?' [106]

The accumulation of evidence above ultimately suggests a form of litmus test, by which we may reasonably verify our conclusion. Genesis 1 must somehow communicate, to an ancient Jewish audience, God's plan to include Gentiles in Jewish promises. This is true no matter how they, or we, would prefer to view the plain account. And this is the impetus of the creation commentary recorded in Deutero-Isaiah. So then either the text of Genesis 1 is an account, from which we may derive an allegory, or alternatively the text itself *is* the allegory.

There is a difference! Just follow the pattern of Sarah and Hagar. If the text is first and foremost a plain account, then the subsequent contradictions we find with respect to spiritual reality may be identified and ignored. If, however, the text is itself an allegory, then the contradictions we find with respect to physical reality are immensely important and must be emphasized. Of course, these contradictions not only exist, but they are numerous!

For example, why does the creation of light on Day 1 precede the creation of the sun on Day 4? God's plan to bring other nations into the promises of Israel starts with a light, which is the appearance of truth, in their darkest hour of captivity. The old heaven and earth stand in ruins. This light came from a great distance, and hovered over the dark waters. All the nations of the earth were present, and waiting, but this earth was "without form, and void". Then much later, as that new creation came into focus, the sun was born. The great bearer of that light, which is Christ, now 'rules' the darkness. 'The true light, which gives light to everyone, was coming into the world. **He was in the world**, and the world was made through him, **yet the world did not know him.**' [107]

---

[106] Romans 9:20
[107] John 1:9, 10

Struggling to explain away the modern, literal inconsistency of light before the sun in the natural world misses the beautiful, spiritual point being made. To assert that the light of Day 1 was not the same as the light of Day 4 ruins the allegory. The 'light, which represents the truth of God's plan for the Gentiles, never changed. Similarly, to assert that the sun was actually created, but hidden, back on Day 1 also ruins the allegory. It is also a logical contradiction. The fact is that the 'light, which represents the truth of God's plan for the Gentiles, clearly should (and does) predate the visible manifestation of Christ. Isaiah had long before told Israel of God's ultimate plan. Therefore, the *only* way to preserve the allegory is to let the text stand as written and avoid forced reconciliation with physical reality. From God's perspective, the creation of light did predate the creation of the sun. And yet, those two different lights sources shine the very same light. This is a spiritual reality, and a physical impossibility.

Thus, God was able to selectively reveal certain aspects of the physical creative process using a literary technique which did not contradict the physical understanding of His ancient audience. God used the imagery of physical creation to represent His spiritual timeline of events, encompassing both the 'former' things of the old covenant and the 'new' things of the new covenant. He was not concerned with forcing agreement between Genesis 1 and any other creation text. Nor was He concerned with forcing agreement between Genesis 1 and modern science, which did not exist at that time.

It is interesting to note, though, that numerous expositors for thousands of years have attempted to allegorize the events of Genesis 1, on top of a plain literal reading, and very many different versions of this have been proposed. However, that is not the conclusion here. Our conclusion, again, is that the text has always been in allegorical format, *and* has already been generally defined for us in Scripture. No speculation is necessary.

So what is literal, and what is nonliteral? Certainly, the author does not wish to establish a false dichotomy. There are very many Biblical passages which describe literal events in nonliteral terms, such as by poetry or song. The events in these cases are literal, but we cannot force every detail of the text to represent historical reality. The use of descriptive language, such as metaphor, may more dramatically communicate a point without being literally true in the plain sense.

Biblical prophecy is another excellent case in point, where symbolic language bridges the gap between a nonliteral text and its literal fulfillment. So it is with allegory. And again, we would underscore the fact that allegorical events described in the Bible are not to be confused with events that are not real, or false, or inaccurate. Neither is a suggestion of this nature intentionally dismissive of the Divine origin of any Biblical text. An allegory simply describes a *different* reality, for a *spiritual* purpose. The allegory of creation is merely the comparison between the real life story and God's spiritual imagery, after the fact.

Our conclusion follows the distinct pattern of interchangeable symbols found in the creation commentary of Deutero-Isaiah. It acknowledges the unique literary features of Genesis 1, as well as the broad use case for the parable genre throughout the Bible. It positions the text as a sequential timeline which emphasizes the physical reality of God as Creator, without enforcing that physical reality to the point that it destroys God's spiritual purpose with the text.

And there are other instances of this elsewhere in the Bible. The story of the Rich Man and Lazarus[108], for example, is a highly relevant analog. Even Jesus was quite content to make specific use of existing, ancient preconceptions, not to affirm them, but rather to teach something else entirely.[109] No modern Christian actually maintains the views of hell and Abraham's Bosom, as precisely understood by the Jewish culture at the time the words were spoken. [110]

---

[108] Luke 16:19-31
[109] Steven Cox, 'The Rich Man, Lazarus, and Abraham', Dec. 2000, <http://www.christadelphia.org/pamphlet/p_lazarus.htm> (16 Mar 2015).
[110] The word ᾅδης (hadēs) here is actually a reference to the Jewish שְׁאוֹל (shĕ'owl), and Christ's description is the Jewish variant of the original Greek concept. Shĕ'owl was an underground abode for all dead, both good and bad. Long before the 1st century CE, the Jewish concept of shĕ'owl had been mingled with Babylonian and Greek mythology. It incorporated multiple, isolated sections, such as the resting place for the righteous

However, Jesus' immediate audience of Pharisees *did* believe in those concepts. They were preconceptions at that time, and Jesus made no effort to speak out against these preconceptions. The factual existence of the mythological locales was irrelevant to the point being made, after all, and the point being made was not understood in the first place. [111] This is why many believers today conclude that the story was a parable. [112]

So the viewpoint of creation as allegory, if it is so, cannot be construed as a 'lie' any more than the story of the Rich Man and Lazarus. The assumed literal components of any allegory or parable are, first and foremost, symbols that communicate spiritual principles. When one accepts that the story of the Rich Man and

---

known as 'Abraham's Bosom'. The original Greek version of hadēs would obviously not contain a place called 'Abraham's Bosom', although some Christian commentators did superimpose this idea upon the Greek myth in NT times, just as the Jews themselves had already done. We cannot be sure that Jesus was able to speak Greek at all, thus the use of the word hadēs appears to be a choice on the part of the writer, which most closely approximated Christ's original intent. In any case, the events described by Jesus significantly conflict with modern mainstream superstitions of the fate of the dead prior to resurrection and judgment. See also Wikipedia contributors. "Bosom of Abraham." Wikipedia, The Free Encyclopedia. Wikipedia, The Free Encyclopedia, 13 Mar. 2015. Web. 16 Mar. 2015.

[111] Many modern Christians often attempt to use this passage to support their belief in a physical place of burning torment for unbelievers. However, it is again emphasized that unless they accept the definition of the terms precisely as the original audience would have understood them, they can no more use this parable to support their modern view than they can use Genesis 1 to support the modern belief in a Divine throne atop the raqiya`. This hadēs is underground, and everyone goes there.

[112] The story in question has been the subject of some historical debate. Some have contended that it is not actually a parable, because it is not characterized upfront in the usual way by the gospel writer, or because it makes use of a personal name. However, very many expositors have concluded that the text is a parable. Perhaps most convincing is the fact that the story appears amidst a series of several other parables, and contains literary similarities common to other parables. Further, the gospels are very clear in stating that Jesus did not speak to the religious hierarchy of his day without the use of parables, for the express purpose of hiding his true meaning. See also Wikipedia contributors. "Rich Man and Lazarus." *Wikipedia, The Free Encyclopedia*. Wikipedia, The Free Encyclopedia, 16 Feb. 2015. Web. 18 Mar. 2015.

Lazarus is a parable, that is to say non literal, they do not contradict the parallel assertion that Lazarus remains a real, historical person. His commitment to Christ and God was factual, and his reward for obedience was believed to be certain.

Finally, whenever God speaks to the creation through poetry or song, throughout Scripture, He declares His plans for future nations of believers. The very concept of this revelation, by whatever method, indicates not a mechanical reenactment of the physical creation, but a purposeful retelling. God is simply instructing us to observe what He did, after the fact, in light of what it means.

And so Genesis 1 is *not* merely the beginning of the story; it is also the end of the story from the Divine vantage point. Per Isaiah and Paul, it illustrates roughly *what* would happen, in symbolic terms which were subsequently explained to the original audience. In the words of Ben Davis, 'My intention here is to add another voice to the conversation by proposing that Genesis 1 functions within its immediate context, as a **theological blueprint** ... **which is not yet complete**.'[113]

---

[113] Ben Davis, 'Genesis 1:1-2:3 As A Theological Blueprint', 2014, < https://www.academia.edu/6675210/GENESIS_1_1-2_3_AS_A_THEOLOGICAL_BLUEPRINT_FOR_GOD_S_CREATION AL_ABODE_A_PROPOSAL> (Nov 2015).

Appendices

I.   The Enigma of Creation

The following collection of citations well illustrates
the utter lack of historical consensus on the text of
Genesis 1, as well as the progress of thought on the
matter, over the course of millennia. Far too many
individuals boldly assume that their particular
opinion is the only reasonable conclusion, when in
fact they have not even bothered to educate
themselves with the realities of the past. We will
discover that both Jewish and Christian
commentators have often struggled with Genesis 1,
stretching the interpretive boundaries that are
incorrectly presumed to exist by many modern
readers.

The Classical Age

Long before Christ's earthly ministry, Jewish rabbis produced
volumes of OT Biblical analysis in the form of oral tradition.
However, due to a variety of factors, most of this valuable historical
data was not redacted and compiled for hundreds of years.
Examples of this oral tradition include the Babylonian and
Jerusalem Talmuds, which date from the third to the sixth century
CE. Therefore, despite the comparatively late Classical Age date of
the written Talmud, we cite it here first. Evangelical author Dr.
Mark Eastman briefly summarizes some of the evidence.

> 'The ancient rabbis reasoned that since God made the
> world in six days and rested on the seventh then the
> world would last seven thousand years. This belief led
> them to speculate about when the Messiah would come
> in relation to the seven thousand years.
>
> In the Babylonian Talmud there is a large section
> (Sanhedrin 96b-99a) in which several prominent rabbis
> express their opinions on the time of the coming of the
> Messiah. Rabbi Elias, who lived 200 years before Jesus

wrote: 'The world endures 6000 years: two thousand
before the law, two thousand with the law and two
thousand with the Messiah.' According to this rabbinical
commentary the Messiah was to come at the end of the
fourth millennium. The Messiah would then be with the
people for two thousand years. After that time, there
would come Messiah's one thousand year reign on earth.
…

The millennium, the one thousand year reign of the
Messiah, is discussed by Rabbi Kattina [as well]: 'The
world endures 6000 years and one thousand it shall be
laid waste, that is, the enemies of God shall be laid
waste, whereof it is said, 'the Lord alone shall be exalted
in that day.' As out of seven years every seventh is a year
of remission, so out of the seven thousand years of the
world, the seventh millennium shall be the 1000 years of
remission, that God alone may be exalted in that day.'
Later in the Sanhedrin we see another reference to the
world week: 'Rabbi Kattina said: six thousand years
shall the world exist, and one thousand it shall be
desolate, as it is written, and the Lord shall alone be
exalted in that day (a reference to Isaiah 2:2). Rabbi
Abaye said: it will be desolate two thousand years, as it
is said, after two days will he revive us: in the third day,
he will raise us up, and we shall live in his sight (a
reference to Hosea 6:1). It has been taught in accordance
with Rabbi Kattina: just as the seventh year is one year
of release in seven, so is the world: one thousand years
out of seven shall be fallow, as it is written and the Lord
shall alone be exalted in that day.'[114]

Rabbi Abba Hillel Silver also explains, in detail, the impact of the
Jewish symbolism derived from the creation timeline in the 1st
century.

'Prior to the first century (C.E.) the Messianic interest
was not excessive...The First Century, however,
especially the generation before the destruction [of the

---

[114] Mark Eastman, *The Search for the Messiah*,
<https://www.blueletterbible.org/Comm/eastman_mark/messiah/sfm_06.cf
m>.

Second Temple] witnessed a remarkable outburst of
Messianic emotionalism.
This is to be attributed, as we shall see, not to an
intensification of Roman persecution, but to the
prevalent belief induced by the popular chronology of
that day that the age was on the threshold of the
Millennium...when Jesus came into Galilee, 'spreading
the gospel of the kingdom of God and saying the 'time is
fulfilled' and the Kingdom of God is at hand,' he was
voicing the opinion universally held that...the age of the
kingdom of God-was at hand...it was this chronological
fact which inflamed the Messianic hope rather than the
Roman persecutions...Jesus appeared in the
procuratorship of Pontius Pilate (26-36 C.E.)...It seems
likely, therefore, that in the minds of the people the
Millennium was to begin around the year 30 C.E. Be it
remembered that it is not the Messiah who brings about
the Millennium. It is the inevitable advent of the
Millennium which carries along with it the Messiah and
his appointed activities. The Messiah was expected
around the second quarter of the First Century C.E.
because the Millennium was at hand. Prior to that time
he was not expected, because according to the
chronology of the day the Millennium was still
considerably removed.'[115]

The 1st century Jewish historian Josephus pointed out that Genesis
1 does not define the first day of creation as '*the*' first day of the
world's history, but rather merely as '*one* day'. Presumably this
strange phrasing would appear to indicate that either the first day of
creation was not the very first day ever, or that the first day of
creation actually took longer than one day to complete. Either way,
he suggested that he was aware of an interpretation by which he
could reconcile this. Although we have no extant record of his
explanation, his testimony is early evidence of observed anomalies
within Genesis 1 from a non-Christian source who nevertheless
accepted the authenticity of the text.

'He named the beginning of light and the time of rest, the
Evening and the Morning; and this was indeed the first
day: **but Moses said it was one day**, - the cause of

---

[115] Abba Hillel Silver, *A History of Messianic Speculation in Israel*,
(MacMillan Co., 1927), 5-7.

which I am able to give even now; but because I have promised to give such reasons for all things in a treatise by itself, I shall put off its exposition till that time.'[116]

'In addition, that difference of expression ('one day' instead of 'first day') was the object of explicit discussion in nearly all ancient commentaries...whether Jewish (e.g. Philo and Rashi) or Christian (e.g. Basil and Augustine). Alas, the difference seems excessively subtle to modern minds, which come to the first chapter of Genesis as though it were a text of astrophysics.'[117]

The non-canonical Epistle of Barnabas, generally placed between the 1st and 2nd centuries, reiterates the Jewish symbolic creation timeline interpretation from the Christian perspective.

> 'Of the Sabbath He speaketh in the beginning of the creation; And God made the works of His hands in six days, and He ended on the seventh day, and rested on it, and He hallowed it. Give heed, children, what this meaneth; He ended in six days. He meaneth this, that in six thousand years the Lord shall bring all things to an end; for the day with Him signifyeth a thousand years; and this He himself beareth me witness, saying; Behold, the day of the Lord shall be as a thousand years. Therefore, children, in six days, that is in six thousand years, everything shall come to an end. And He rested on the seventh day. this He meaneth; when His Son shall come, and shall abolish the time of the Lawless One, and shall judge the ungodly, and shall change the sun and the moon and the stars, then shall he truly rest on the seventh day.'[118]

Irenaeus, a 2nd century apologist, argued in favor of literal creation days as well as the symbolic creation timeline in his famous work *Against Heresies*.

---

[116] William Whiston trans., *Josephus: The Complete Works*, (Thomas Nelson Publishers, 1998), 33. Emphasis mine. See Antiquities 1.1.1.
[117] Patrick Reardon, *Creation And The Patriarchal Histories*, (Ancient Faith Publishing, 2008), 32-33.
[118] J.B. Lightfoot, trans., *Epistle of Barnabas* Chapter XV, <http://www.earlychristianwritings.com/text/barnabas-lightfoot.html>.

'For in as many days as this world was made, in so many thousand years shall it be concluded. And for this reason the Scripture says: "Thus the heaven and the earth were finished, and all their adornment. And God brought to a conclusion upon the sixth day the works that He had made; and God rested upon the seventh day from all His works." This is an account of the things formerly created, as also it is a prophecy of what is to come. For the day of the Lord is as a thousand years; and in six days created things were completed: it is evident, therefore, that they will come to an end at the sixth thousand year'[119]

Origen, one of the best known philosophers of the 3rd century, disagreed with men like Irenaeus. Apart from the influence of modern science, he assumed that rational problems exist in Genesis 1 when it is read in a strictly literal sense.

'We should not believe that any other thing could be understood in the Scriptures save what was obvious, the word of God has arranged that certain stumbling-blocks, as it were, and offenses, and impossibilities, should be introduced...And this also we must know, that the principal aim being to announce the spiritual connection in those things that are done, and that ought to be done, where the Word found that things done according to the history could be adapted to these mystical senses, He made use of them, concealing from the multitude the deeper meaning; ... the Scripture interwove in the history (the account of) some event that did not take place, sometimes what could not have happened; sometimes what could, but did not. And sometimes a few words are interpolated which are not true in their literal acceptation, and sometimes a larger number....He did the same thing both with the evangelists and the apostles—as even these do not contain throughout a pure history of events, which are interwoven indeed according to the letter, but which did not actually occur. Nor even do the law and the commandments wholly convey what is agreeable to reason. For who that has understanding will suppose that the first, and second, and

---

[119] Irenaeus, *Against Heresies* Book V Chapter XXVIII, <http://www.newadvent.org/fathers/0103528.htm>.

third day, and the evening and the morning, existed
without a sun, and moon, and stars? And that the first
day was, as it were, also without a sky? ... The attentive
reader may notice in the Gospels innumerable other passages like these, so that he will be convinced that in the
histories that are literally recorded, circumstances that
did not occur are inserted.'[120]

Lactantius, a 3rd and 4th century author and advisor to Emperor
Constantine I, was not concerned, as Origen, with the apparent
difficulties in the way of a literal reading of the days of creation. At
the same time however, he followed the lead of the oral Jewish
tradition by asserting a connection between the creation days and
the events of human history. He stated, 'Therefore, since all the
works of God were completed in six days, the world must continue
in its present state through six ages, that is, six thousand years. For
the great day of God is limited by a circle of a thousand years, as the
prophet shows, who says 'In Thy sight, O Lord, a thousand years
are as one day.' And as God laboured during those six days in
creating such great works, so His religion and truth must labour
during these six thousand years, while wickedness prevails and
bears rule.'[121]

Baptist apologist Bernard Ramm notes regarding Augustine, the
leading theologian of the 4th and 5th centuries, that '[he] does not
call them geological days, and it has been argued that there is
nothing in Augustine to justify any belief in a period of time for
these days. The point Augustine actually makes is that the creation
days are so great, so majestic, so profound that we cannot consider
them as mere sun-divided days but as God-divided days. They are
creative days, not solar days, and so he calls them *natures, growths,
dies ineffabiles.*'[122] This is confirmed by Thomas Aquinas, where
he states concerning Augustine that 'his opinion is that all the days
that are called seven, are one day represented in a sevenfold aspect
(Gen. ad lit. iv, 22; De Civ. Dei xi, 9; Ad Orosium xxvi). [123]

---

[120] Origen, *First Principles* Book IV Chapter XV-XVI,
<http://www.newadvent.org/fathers/04124.htm>.
[121]Lactantius, *The Divine Institutes Book VII Chapter XIV*,
<http://www.ccel.org/ccel/schaff/anf07.iii.ii.vii.xiv.html>.
[122]Bernard Ramm, *The Christian View of Science and Scripture*, (Grand
Rapids: Eerdmans, 1954), 147.

Augustine was also the first leading Christian to expressly outline, in detail, the symbolic timeline interpretation which both Christians and Jews had professed before him. That is, that the days of creation were purposefully intended to represent, in succession, periods of earth's history, or 'ages'.

> 'Five ages of the world, accordingly, having been now completed (there has entered the sixth). Of these ages the first is from the beginning of the human race, that is, from Adam, who was the first man that was made, down to Noah, who constructed the ark at the time of the flood. Then the second extends from that period on to Abraham ... from which people also Christ the Saviour was decreed to come according to the flesh. For these turning-points of those two ages occupy an eminent place in the ancient books. On the other hand, those of the other three ages are also declared in the Gospel, where the descent of the Lord Jesus Christ according to the flesh is likewise mentioned. For the third age extends from Abraham on to David the king; the fourth from David on to that captivity whereby the people of God passed over into Babylonia; and the fifth from that transmigration down to the advent of our Lord Jesus Christ. With His coming the sixth age has entered on its process; so that now the spiritual grace, which in previous times was known to a few patriarchs and prophets, may be made manifest to all nations... in order that in this sixth age the mind of man may be renewed after the image of God, even as on the sixth day man was made after the image of God.'[124]

Author Robert Bradshaw has produced an excellent and concise summary titled 'Creationism and the Early Church'. In his book he documents a wide range of opinion on the creation timeline over a 400 year period; his outline table of results is reproduced here for reference.[125]

---

[123] Fathers of the English Dominican Province, trans., *Summa Theologica, Pt. 1: Q74, Article 2,* <http://www.ccel.org/ccel/aquinas/summa/FP/FP074.html#FPQ74A3THEP1>.

[124] Augustine, *On the Catechising of the Uninstructed Chapter XXII,* <*http://www.newadvent.org/fathers/1303.htm*>.

[125] Robert Bradshaw, *Creationism and the Early Church,*

Writer	Date	24 hours	Figurative	Unclear	Reference
Philo	c.20 BC- c.AD 50		X		*Creation* 13
Josephus	AD 37/38- c.100			X	*Antiquities* 1.1.1 (1.27-33)
Justin Martyr	c.100 - c.165			X	
Tatian	110-180			X	
Theophilus of Antioch	c.180	X			*Autolycus* 2.11-12
Irenaeus of Lyons	c.115-202			X	
Clement of Alexandria	c.150 - c.215		X		*Miscellanies* 6.16
Tertullian	c.160 - c.225			X	
Julius Africanus	c.160-240			X	
Hippolytus of Rome	170-236			X	*Genesis*, 1.5
Origen	185-253		X		*Celsus*, 6.50, 60
Methodius	d.311	X			*Chastity* 5.7
Lactantius	240-320	X			*Institutes* 7.14
Victorinus of Pettau	d. c. 304	X			*Creation*
Eusebius of Caesarea	263-339			X	
Ephrem the Syrian	306-373	X			*Commentary on Genesis* 1.1
Epiphanius of Salamis	315-403	X			*Panarion*, 1.1.1
Basil of Caesarea	329-379	X			*Hexaemeron*, 2.8
Gregory of	330-394			X	

Nyssa					
Gregory of Nazianxus	330-390			X	
Cyril of Jerusalem	d. 387	X			*Catechetical Lectures* 12.5
Ambrose of Milan	339-397	X			*Hexaemeron,* 1.10.3-7
John Chrysostom	374-407			X	
Jerome	347-419/420			X	
Augustine of Hippo	354-430		X		*Literal,* 4.22.39

Table 13: The Length Of The Creation Days

Bradshaw states in the opening summary of his work that 'early drafts of my manuscript clearly indicate my intention - to demonstrate that the early church fathers were forerunners of the modern young earth creationists. As time passed this began to change and I began to gain a greater appreciation for the writings of the fathers' themselves. The final result is *not* a wholesale endorsement of the young earth creationist position, but I hope, *an accurate summary of diversity of opinion that existed during the formative centuries of Christianity.*[126]

So then we see, 'The history of interpretation of Genesis 1-3 is **anything but monolithic, and neither doctrine nor exegesis is characterized by complete homogeneity**. This fact can be observed even in the earliest periods.'[127] 'One feature becomes clear from even a cursory study of this period [the first couple centuries after Christ]: **we do not find a univocal reading or a single method** ... We do, however, find a consistent and coherent pattern of reading, whose theological character is considerably different from the modern mainstream.'[128]

---

[126]*Ibid,* <http://www.robibradshaw.com/summary.htm>. Emphasis mine.

[127] John Walton, *The Lost World of Adam and Eve*, (InterVarsity Press, 2015), 2. Emphasis mine.

[128] Peter Bouteneff, *Beginnings: Ancient Christian Readings of the Biblical Creation Narratives*, (Baker Academic, Grand Rapids MI, 2008), ix.

With specific regard to the creation timeline, we see that the literal view of the days of creation tended to be uncertain while the basic symbolic function of the days was not! Even when expositors in this time period would refer to the 'days' per se, they were not always clear whether or not they meant it in a sense that would convey a nominal, 24 hour duration. This seems quite strange, and counterintuitive, but nonetheless it is true. Further, we note that the symbolic creation timeline was essentially lifted by the first Christians right out of Jewish rabbinical thought.

The Medieval Age

The passage of time did nothing but exaggerate the difficulties and questions surrounding the text of Genesis 1. Although the medieval age was not particularly known for its academic advancements, the general approach to Biblical interpretation was not altogether unaffected by trends in scholarship. Indeed, the medieval ages show that Jewish expositors were much more inclined to follow the cutting edge, as opposed to their Christian counterparts, being willing to accept that the Classical explanation of the literal creation mechanics was not an explanation at all. In parallel, the acceptance of the symbolic creation timeline did not diminish in the least, but rather continued to flourish.

The 8th century Catholic doctor and historian Bede followed closely in the footsteps of Augustine, also enumerating the creation days as an allegory for ages of the history of the earth.

> 'Hitherto it may have sufficed to speak literally of the origins of the growing world. It is pleasing, however, to intimate in a few words that order of those six or seven days in which the world was made correspond to its ages - which are of the same number. For the first day, on the which God said, 'Let there be light, and there was light', corresponds with the first age in whose beginning that same world was made and man was set in the pleasurable delights of paradise, where he enjoyed the presence of his maker's grace, free, and innocent of all evil. But that day already began to decline towards evening when the

Emphasis mine.

first people lost, by sinning, the happiness of the heavenly homeland and were sent into this vale of tears...On the second day the firmament was made in the midst of the waters, and in the second age of the world, the ark, in which the remains of the human race and the seed of succeeding ages, so to speak, was preserved, was placed in the midst of the waters...On the seventh day God rested from all his works, and sanctified and blessed it; and the seventh age is eternal rest in another life, in which God rests with his saints in eternity after the good works, which He accomplished in them throughout the six ages of this world.'[129]

Dr. Jeffrey Tigay, Professor of Hebrew and Semitic Languages at the University of Pennsylvania, clearly illustrates that preeminent Jewish scholars of the 10th and 12th centuries were not prepared to isolate their view of the Biblical creation from natural reality.

'In the Middle Ages, Saadia Gaon argued that a Biblical passage should not be interpreted literally if that made a passage mean something contrary to the senses or reason (or, as we would say, science; **Emunotve-Deot**, chap. 7). Maimonides applied this principle to theories about the creation. He held that if the eternity of the universe (what we would call the Steady State theory) could be proven by logic (science) then the Biblical passages speaking about creation at a point in time could and should be interpreted figuratively in a way that is compatible with the eternity of the universe. It is only because the eternity of the universe has not been proven that he interpreted the verses about creation at a point in time literally (**Guide**, II, 25), but he still insisted that the creation story as a whole was written metaphorically (Book I, Introduction). To Saadia and Maimonides, belief in the truth of the Bible does not re-quire a denial of science ('reason,' 'logic') when the two seem to conflict. These philosophers imply that questions of science should be left to scientists and scientific method. In fact, Maimonides quotes a passage in the Talmud in which Jewish scholars abandoned an astronomical theory of their own in favor of a theory of

---

[129] Verity Allan, trans., *In Genesim I.1093-1224,* <*http://tartarus.org/verity/Bede_ug.pdf*>, *27-31.*

gentile scholars (Pes. 94b). Maimonides approved of their action, saying that 'speculative matters every one treats according to the results of his own study, and everyone accepts that which appears to him established by proof' (**Guide**, II, 8).'[130]

The French rabbi Rashi is accepted by Jews even today as a preeminent authority on textual interpretation. He wrote in the 11th century regarding the Hebrew grammar of Genesis 1:1, which he believed to support a non-literal interpretation of the entire creation chronology.

'This verse calls for a midrashic interpretation. ... Scripture did not come to teach the sequence of the Creation, to say that these came first, for if it came to teach this, it should have written:'At first (בָּרִאשׁוֹנָה) He created the heavens and the earth,' for there is no רֵאשִׁית in Scripture that is not connected to the following word, [i.e., in the construct state] like (ibid. 27:1):'In the beginning of (בְּרֵאשִׁית) the reign of Jehoiakim' ; (below 10:10)'the beginning of (רֵאשִׁית) his reign' ; (Deut. 18:4)'the first (רֵאשִׁית) of your corn.' Here too, you say בָּרָא אֱלֹהִים בְּרֵאשִׁית, like בְּרֵאשִׁית בְּרֹא, in the beginning of creating. And similar to this is,'At the beginning of the Lord's speaking (דִּבֶּר) to Hosea,' (Hos. 1:2), i.e., at the beginning of the speaking (וּרְדֻבַּר) of the Holy One, Blessed be He, to Hosea, 'the Lord said to Hosea, etc.... [if you say that Scripture indicates the order of creation] be astounded at yourself, for the water preceded, as it is written: 'and the spirit of God hovered over the face of the water,' and Scripture did not yet disclose when the creation of water took place!... Perforce, you must admit that Scripture did not teach us anything about the sequence of the earlier and the later [acts of creation].[131]

The influential Hugh of St. Victor had a particular interest in Genesis 1 during the 12th century, and his writings were distributed

---

[130] Jeffrey Tigay, *Genesis, Science, and 'Scientific Creationism'*, <http://www.sas.upenn.edu/~jtigay/sci.htm>.
[131]Rashi, *'Commentary on Genesis'*, <http://www.chabad.org/library/bible_cdo/aid/8165#showrashi=true>. 10 Aug 2015.

all throughout Europe. He was a proponent of a type of blended, one day – six day creation view.

> 'God certainly could have created everything at once, says Hugh in *De sacramentis*, but chose to use the six day format 'for the instruction of and the example for' the rational creature who can learn something from this, namely the angels originally and the human readers of scripture later. Hugh can also reconcile simultaneity with six days, both with scriptural and patristic support, by assigning simultaneity to the creation of all raw matter at once, and then the progression of six days to the granting of form to this original matter. …Hugh did not completely restrict himself to a literal-historical reading of the text. … 'It was for the repair of the human that God wished to distribute His work over six days,' so that the human might learn to progress from plain being to blessed being. …Hugh's extant work show minimal interest both in creation by itself and also in the literal-historical sense by itself, although it is the foundation. These works show maximal interest in restoration and in the two senses of Scripture that build upon the historical foundation, namely the allegorical-doctrinal sense, as seen shortly in *De sacramentis,* and the tropological or spiritual (moral) sense, as evident at length in a wide array of works.'[132]

As it turns out the, the controversy over whether or not the creation took place over the course of one day was so significant that Thomas Aquinas addressed it in his 13th century apologetics work, Summa Theologica. He cites four common assertions in favor of the single day viewpoint, and although he argues against them, his work is a testament to this popular disagreement.

> 'Objection 1: It would seem that all these days are one day. For it is written (Gn. 2:4,5): 'These are the generations of the heaven and the earth, when they were created, in the day that the Lord . . . made the heaven and the earth, and every plant of the field, before it sprung up in the earth.' Therefore the day in which God made 'the heaven and the earth, and every plant of the field,' is one and the same day. But He made the heaven and the earth

---

[132] Paul Rorem, *Hugh of St. Victor*, (Oxford University Press, 2009), 54-55.

on the first day, or rather before there was any day, but the plant of the field He made on the third day. Therefore the first and third days are but one day, and for a like reason all the rest.

Objection 2: Further, it is said (Ecclus. 18:1): 'He that liveth forever, created all things together.' But this would not be the case if the days of these works were more than one. Therefore they are not many but one only.

Objection 3: Further, on the seventh day God ceased from all new works. If, then, the seventh day is distinct from the other days, it follows that He did not make that day; which is not admissible.

Objection 4: Further, the entire work ascribed to one day God perfected in an instant, for with each work are the words (God) 'said . . . . and it was . . . done.' If, then, He had kept back His next work to another day, it would follow that for the remainder of a day He would have ceased from working and left it vacant, which would be superfluous. The day, therefore, of the preceding work is one with the day of the work that follows.'[133]

The Protestant Reformation was a time in which a greater emphasis on the literal aspects of Genesis 1 saw popular resurgence. This was in direct opposition to the traditional Catholic tendency to emphasize the symbolic meanings taught by the Church fathers, whether the days of creation themselves were believed to be literal or not. Martin Luther, the founder of the movement in the 16th century, vigorously defended this view against the teachings of men like Augustine in the Classical Age and Hugh of St. Victor in the Medieval Age by stating, 'When Moses writes that God created heaven and earth and whatever is in them in six days, then let this period continue to have been six days, and do not venture to devise any comment according to which six days were one day. But, if you cannot understand how this could have been done in six days, then grant the Holy Spirit the honor of being more learned than you are.'[134]

---

[133] Fathers of the English Dominican Province, trans., *Summa Theologica, Pt. 1: Q74, Article 2*, <http://www.ccel.org/ccel/aquinas/summa/FP/FP074.html#FPQ74A3THEP1>.

Luther also stubbornly demanded that the Bible student accept the literal view of creation, irrespective of what one may naturally observe. 'Scripture simply says that the moon, the sun, and the stars were placed in the firmament of the heaven, below and above which heaven are the waters... It is likely that the stars are fastened to the firmament like globes of fire, to shed light at night... We Christians must be different from the philosophers in the way we think about the causes of things. And if some are beyond our comprehension like those before us concerning the waters above the heavens, we must believe them rather than wickedly deny them or presumptuously interpret them in conformity with our understanding.'[135]

Despite the disputed literal readings, Luther and his powerful Reformation counterpart John Calvin affirmed both Jewish and Catholic teaching by perpetuating the symbolic creation timeline interpretation derived from the days in Genesis 1.

> 'We must not be moved by the profane jeer, that it is strange how it did not sooner occur to the Deity to create the heavens and the earth, instead of idly allowing an infinite period to pass away, during which thousands of generations might have existed, while the present world is drawing to a close before it has completed its six thousandth year. Why God delayed so long it is neither fit nor lawful to inquire. ... as if the ample circumference of heaven and earth did not contain objects numerous and resplendent enough to absorb all our senses; as if, in the period of six thousand years, God had not furnished facts enough to exercise our minds in ceaseless meditation ... With the same view Moses relates that the work of creation was accomplished not in one moment, but in six days. By this statement we are drawn away from fiction to the one God who thus divided his work into six days, that we may have no reluctance to devote our whole lives to the contemplation of it.'[136]

---

[134] Ewald M. Plass, compiler, *What Luther Says. A Practical In-Home Anthology for the Active Christian*, (Concordia, 1959), 93.
[135] Janoslaw Pelican, editor, *Martin Luther. Luther's Works, Vol. 1. Lectures on Genesis*, (Concordia, 1958), 30, 42, 43.
[136] John Calvin, *Institutes of the Christian Religion* Book XIV, <http://www.ntslibrary.com/PDF%20Books/Calvin%20Institutes%20of%2

If it had not yet been made clear to the reader, it most certainly should have by now. Genesis 1 has seen a very long history of dispute. Surprisingly, the symbolic interpretation of the days of creation continued throughout the Medieval Age to be the single, constant source of agreement for essentially all expositors. Particularly with respect to medieval Jewish thought, it has been said that 'elaborating on the theme of the seventh millennium representing the Messianic Age are numerous early and late Jewish scholars, including the Ramban, Isaac Abrabanel, Abraham Ibn Ezra, Rabbeinu Bachya, [and] the Vilna Gaon... The acceptance of the idea of the seventh millennium representing the Messianic Age across the Ashkenazi - Sephardi divide, the Chassidim - Misnagdim divide, and across the rational Talmud and mystical Kabbalah perspectives, shows on the centrality of this idea in traditional Judaism.'[137]

The Pre-Modern Age

The now mature piety of the Reformation scholars collided violently with the realities of new discovery in the Pre-Modern Age. Far from reconciliation, the interpretive model of the creation literally devolved into chaos. Substantial attempts were made by expositors in this time period to reinvent the interpretation of Genesis 1, so as not to lose faith or credibility. Even the symbolic creation timeline began to show evidence of weakness. The cornerstone of creation consensus itself, while still enjoying broad support, deteriorated rapidly near the end of the Pre-Modern Age.

Concerning the 17th century, and Sir Isaac Newton, Dr. Reiner Smolinksi is quoted here extensively. His account is exemplary of this pivotal period in the historical record.

> 'Even the great Sir Isaac Newton (1642-1727) struggled with the problem of creation chronometry. In an extant fragment dating to 24 December 1680, he debated the

---

0Christian%20Religion.pdf>.
[137] Wikipedia contributors. 'Year 6000.' *Wikipedia, The Free Encyclopedia*. Wikipedia, The Free Encyclopedia, 25 Sep. 2014. Web. 28 Nov. 2014.

issue with Thomas Burnet, his old friend in Cambridge, just months before Burnet published his divisive *TellurisTheoria Sacra*. ...Newton had written to Burnet that the six days of creation were not each merely twenty-four hours in duration but considerably longer because the earth's diurnal revolution at that time could 'have been very slow, soeyt ye first 6 revolutions or days might containe time enough for ye whole Creation.' Burnet had penetrated the underlying logic of his friend's self-serving argument but pretended to be puzzled by Newton's intriguing solution-introducing shifting concepts of time before time began. In his letter of 13 January 1680/81, Burnet rejoined, 'I inferr from this, yt as ye distinction of 6 dayes is noe physical reality soe neither is this draught of the creation [Moses' hexaemeron] physical but Ideal, or if you will, morall. Seeing it is not physically true yt ye Sun Moon & Stars were made at yt time, viz. 5 or 6ooo yeares since when ye Earth was form'd. And if it bee Ideal in one part, it may in some proportion bee ideal in every part.' Sir Isaac, Burnet was quick to underscore, had thereby allegorized the Creation, thus snatching it out of the realm of scientific consideration.

Newton, however, would not concede that he had offered a wax-nosed interpretation. In responding to Burnet, he reclaimed his scientific credentials. 'You may make ye first day as long as you please,' he patiently explained, '& ye second day too if there was no diurnal motion till there was a terraqueous globe, that is till towards ye end of that days work. And then if you will suppose ye earth put in motion by an eaven force applied to it, & that ye first revolution was done in one of our years,' the earth could have achieved 365 revolutions in 'the 183d year.' Despite his best attempts, however, Newton was clearly becoming mired in the quicksand of his own mechanistic conjecture and felt compelled to return to the safe ground of divine teleology. Natural causation alone could not sufficiently account for the earth's diurnal motion, he emphasized, for none but 'God gave the earth it's [sic] motion by such degrees & at such times as was most suitable to ye creatures.' Paradoxically, by resorting to supernatural agency when the going got rough, Sir Isaac appears to be disavowing the Enlightenment cosmogony that dares to speak his name: Newtonianism, a concept that among his Deist disciples came to signify a rationalist and mechanistic universe devoid of miracles.

Justifiably apprehensive of ecclesiastical backlash, Newton did not rush in where angels fear to tread. Deeply religious, he desperately clung to the Bible as God's revealed Word. But to resort to dogmatism was out of the question; to miracles, only in extraordinary cases. It was much easier for him to sacrifice the letter as long as the spirit of the hexaemeron was preserved. Newton's response to Burnet's epistle is highly revealing and deserves to be quoted at length:

'As to Moses I do not think his description of ye creation either Philosophical or feigned, but that he described realities in a language artificially adapted to ye sense of ye vulgar. Thus where he speaks of two great lights [Gen. 1:16] I suppose he means their apparent, not real greatness. So when he tells us God placed those lights in ye firmament, he speaks I suppose of their apparent not of their real place.... So when he tells us of two great lights & the starrs made ye 4th day, I do not think their creation from beginning to end was done ye fourth day nor in any one day of ye creation nor that Moses mentions their creation as they were physicall bodies in themselves some of them greater then [sic] this earth & perhaps habitable worlds, but only as they were lights to this earth.'

Newton thus ingeniously saves the day by distinguishing between the 'real' (literal) creation outside time and ken of man, and its 'apparent' (visible) manifestation as it might appear to an eyewitness on earth 'if he had then lived & were now de scribing what he saw.' The formation of the two great lights spoken of in Gen. 1: 16 therefore did not take place on the fourth day; instead, at that time, they simply became visible to the naked eye through the mist of the earth's hazy atmosphere. The Mosaic creation of the fourth day was thus no more than an optical illusion.

Newton's phenomenological solution thus amounts to a 'middle way' between the grammatical and allegorical sense of scripture, a didactic narrative of events that Moses adapted to the needs of the uneducated masses

recently freed from Egyptian slavery. Newton explains,
'Omit them he [Moses] could not without rendering his
description of ye creation imperfect in ye judgment of ye
vulgar. To describe them distinctly as they were in
themselves would have made ye narration tedious &
confused, amused ye vulgar & become a Philosopher
more then [sic] a Prophet.He mentions them therefore
only so far as ye vulgar had a notion of them, that is as
they were phaenomena in our firmament, & describes
their making only so far & at such a time as they were
made such phaenomena.'

Sir Isaac's strategy of accommodation, then, is at once
philosophically plausible and theologically sound, yet it
also discloses how he wrestled with angels to make the
Mosaic hexaemeron safe for the early Enlightenment's
new science.'[138]

On the heels of explosive scientific advancements, the early
American Puritan minister Cotton Mather spent his entire ministry
struggling with the task of reconciling the secular evidence with
Scripture in the 17th and 18th centuries. He wrote much about this in
his voluminous '*Biblia Americana*', as noted again by Dr.
Smolinksi.

'The variety of authors Mather included in his 'Biblia
Americana' is as revealing as his critique of their
theories, for the spectrum of views he considered
suggests the degree to which he was willing to allow
biblical authority to be questioned as he explored early
Enlightenment science in the work he thought the
crowning achievement of his life. In treating the Mosaic
hexaemeron-in more than seventy folio pages in double
columns (55r-129r)-Mather sampled ancient
cosmogonies, early Enlightenment science, and
philological and textual disputes about the authorship of
the Pentateuch. During his lifetime, the biblical creation
story was experiencing unprecedented challenges, with
Peripatetics pitting their theory of the eternity of the

---

[138] Reiner Smolinksi, 'How to Go to Heaven, or How Heaven Goes?
Natural Science and Interpretation in Cotton Mather's *'Biblia Americana'*
(1693-1728)', *The New England Quarterly*, Vol. 81, No. 2 (Jun., 2008),
296-300.

universe against those conservative physico theologians who insisted that God had created the universe out of nothing, with Copernican heliocentrism replacing the ancient Ptolemaic geocentric cosmogonies, and with Cartesian mechanism and the immutable laws of nature contesting the venerable miracles and providentialist views of conventional literalists. The sudden explosion of knowledge and the formation of new fields of inquiry-physics, chemistry, botany, geology disrupted the usual progress of biblical exegesis and demanded the attention of the brightest and the best. …

In pondering the possibilities, Mather [says] How could the celestial bodies proceeding from a single center traverse such 'Immense Distances' as to arrive at their 'vastly Remote Seats' in outer space in so short a time as 'a few Hours' of the First Day,.. as he critiques the standard creation story, especially if the centripetal force of universal gravitation (Newton's Second Law of Motion) pulls all moving bodies toward 'the common Center of Gravity'? Even if a thousand years were allowed for each of the six days of Creation, the magnetic property of matter would countermand the velocity of bodies wafting across space, Mather muses. …

Suddenly, the tidy arrangement of the Mosaic hexaemeron, no doubt pleasing in its poetic simplicity, seemed strangely out moded and inadequate when examined within the context of the new theories. Though sacrosanct among the faithful for millennia, the old Mosaic order strained the credulity of physico theologians like Mather as they wrestled with the problem of squaring religion and science according to one common denominator. …

'Now, tho' God Almighty can do all things in what Portions of Time Hee pleases,' Mather readily concedes, 'Man cannot. Hee must have Time allow'd him, in Proportion to the Business, that is to bee done. But behold here, Business enough allotted into the Sixth Day, to require no small Part of a Year, for the Dispatch of it!' ('Biblia Americana,' p. 72v). Even if Adam were created in a state of maturity and with full knowledge and understanding of his assigned tasks, their sheer number would encompass a lifetime, not a day. How, then, can a rational explanation be devised if God's creation is constrained by his own physical laws? 'It is an Indecent Thing to Recurr unto Pure Miracle, for the Acceleration of them, into the Space of Twenty Four Hours,' Mather affirms with reference to Whiston, violates 'the Lawes of Motion, [which] were now already Stated and Fixed in the World' ('Biblia Americana,' p. 72v)

Signs of storm and stress are visible throughout 'Biblia Americana' when Mather moves beyond the grand outline of the Mosaic creation story, which (he reluctantly admits) is not intended to be a scientifically accurate explanation in the first place but merely an account of what an eyewitnesses might have seen or what Moses or any other prophet might have adapted to the simple understanding of an illiterate people.' [139]

Of particular note, the 18th century English historian Edward Gibbon confirms that the notion of the symbolic creation timeline was first attributed, in its pre Christian form, to the Jewish rabbis who claimed to be of the 'school of Elijah' the prophet.

'The ancient and popular doctrine of the Millennium was intimately connected with the second coming of Christ. As the works of the creation had been finished in six days, **their duration in their present state, according to a tradition which was attributed to the prophet Elijah, was fixed to six thousand years.** By the same analogy it was inferred, that this long period of labor and contention, which was now almost elapsed, would be succeeded by a joyful Sabbath of a thousand years; and that Christ, with the triumphant band of the saints and the elect who had escaped death, or who had been miraculously revived, would reign upon earth till the time appointed for the last and general resurrection. ... The assurance of such a Millennium was carefully inculcated by a succession of fathers from Justin Martyr, and Irenæus, who conversed with the immediate disciples of the apostles, down to Lactantius, who was preceptor to the son of Constantine. **Though it might**

---

[139] Ibid, 286, 289-292, 307.

**not be universally received, it appears to have been
the reigning sentiment of the orthodox believers**; and
it seems so well adapted to the desires and apprehensions
of mankind, that it must have contributed in a very
considerable degree to the progress of the Christian
faith.'[140]

In his widely read, early 18th century commentary, the Non-
Conformist minister Matthew Henry was unaffected by the findings
of contemporary science and maintained a literal, young earth view.

'The foundation of all religion being laid in our relation
to God as our Creator, it was fit that the book of divine
revelations… should begin, as it does, with a plain and
full account of the creation of the world…. Concerning
this the pagan philosophers wretchedly blundered, and
became vain in their imaginations, some asserting the
world's eternity and self-existence, others ascribing it to a
fortuitous concourse of atoms: thus 'the world by
wisdom knew not God,' but took a great deal of pains to
lose him. The Holy Scripture therefore…by revealed
religion [designed] to maintain and improve natural
religion… The evening and the morning were the sixth
day; so that in six days God made the world. We are not
to think but that God could have made the world in an
instant. He said that, Let there be light, and there was
light, could have said, 'Let there be a world,' and there
would have been a world, in a moment, in the twinkling
of an eye, as at the resurrection, 1 Co. 15:52. But he did
it in six days, that he might show himself a free-agent,
doing his own work both in his own way and in his own
time,-that his wisdom, power, and goodness, might
appear to us, and be meditated upon by us, the more
distinctly,-and that he might set us an example of
working six days and resting the seventh; it is therefore
made the reason of the fourth commandment. So much
would the Sabbath conduce to the keeping up of religion
in the world that God had an eye to it in the timing of his
creation.'[141]

---

[140] Edward Gibbon, *The Decline and Fall of The Roman Empire: Vol. I,
Ch. XV, Pt. IV*, < http://www.gutenberg.org/files/890/890-h/890-
h.htm#linkch15-p4>.
[141] Matthew Henry, *The Exposition of the Old and New Testaments*,

The great 19th century Baptist preacher, Charles Spurgeon, did not hesitate to accept that ancient perspectives on the age of the earth, and the supposed dates of creation, were entirely wrong. He supported an old earth view, in the form of the 'gap-theory', as summarized below.

> 'Can any man tell me when the beginning was? Years ago we thought the beginning of this world was when Adam came upon it; but we have discovered that thousands of years before that God was preparing chaotic matter to make it a fit abode for man, putting races of creatures upon it, who might die and leave behind the marks of his handiwork and marvelous skill, before he tried his hand on man. But that was not the beginning, for revelation points us to a period long ere this world was fashioned, to the days when the morning stars were begotten; when, like drops of dew, from the fingers of the morning, stars and constellations fell trickling from the hand of God; when, by his own lips, he launched forth ponderous orbs; when with his own hand he sent comets, like thunderbolts, wandering through the sky, to find one day their proper sphere.'[142]

At this point, our initial premise has been made very clear. Although our historical review has not been exhaustive, it is obvious that a multiplicity of views on Genesis 1 have *always* existed, from ancient times. So then, it is simply not rational for the modern reader to forcibly require a particular literal reading from their fellow Bible students. Any literal reading, so called, is in some sense subjective. The reader may not even be aware of all their literal options!

> 'Concordism, generally, is the supposition that the biblical and non-biblical data on a given topic can and should be harmonized ... Two popular-level books that use concordism as broad categories to then subdivide particular views further are Haarsma and Haarsma's *Origins* (Faith Alive, 2011) and Gerald

---

<http://www.blueletterbible.org/Comm/mhc/Gen/Gen_001.cfm?a=1001>.
[142] Charles Spurgeon, 'Sermon 41-42: Election', < http://www.oldearth.org/spurgeon/spurgeon_sermon_41-42.htm>.

> Rau's *Mapping the Origins Debate: Six Models of the Beginning of Everything* (InterVarsity, 2012). Haarsma and Haarsma use a concordist-vs.-non-concordist construct: concordist positions include young-earth, gap, day-age, and appearance-of-age interpretations....' [143]

We see that well known Jewish and Christian commentators have viewed from nearly every possible angle a passage that constitutes a fractional percentage of the total Bible. These views may or may not apply subsequent layers of meaning, and they may or may not have important cultural and religious implications for Jewish people living in the Ancient Near East. But all of those we have quoted were firmly convinced in their own minds, and in their own time, that their particular, reasoned solution to the variety of intellectual problems imposed by Genesis 1 was sufficient to preserve the authenticity and authority of the text. Nevertheless, when considered together, this company of witnesses actually testifies to the grand and confused melting pot that is the text of Genesis 1.

---

[143] Ken Turner and Brian Eisenback, 'Discordant Views On Concordism', 23 Feb 2015, < http://biologos.org/blog/discordant-views-on-concordism> (14 March 2015).

II.   What Was The Raqia'?

This paper briefly examines the historical controversy surrounding the physical creation of the raqia' or 'heaven', as described in Genesis 1. This paper also analyzes a specific, spiritual use case for the 'heaven', which requires an ancient perspective on cosmology. In short, the Hebrew word raqia' is an important piece of Biblical evidence which guides our understanding of the creation texts, and will not allow them to be forcibly interpreted from a modern, scientific perspective.

In Genesis 1, the Hebrew word עִיקָר _raqia` is used seven times.[144] According to Scripture it is named by God as שָׁמַיִם shamayim (heaven), and it forms the barrier between the 'waters above' and the 'waters below'. It has been the focus of much debate for thousands of years. Specifically, the perplexing question as to the literal, physical nature of this raqia` has troubled the minds of historical philosophers and theologians to no end.

> 'The basic meaning of the noun is determined by a consideration of the verb raqa'. Here the basic idea is 'to spread out,' and specifically the spreading out of the earth at creation (cf. Ps. 136:6; Isa. 42:5; 44:24) or the spreading out of the sky (cf. Job 37:18). In Isa. 40:19 the meaning is to overlay or plate (with gold). A raqia', then, is something that is created by being spread out either by stretching (e.g., a tent) or by hammering (e.g., a metal; cf. Deut. 28:23, in which the sky in a time of drought is likened to bronze; cf. also the use of raqa' in Exod. 39:3, where the meaning is clearly 'to hammer out'.[145]

Author Paul Seely, in his well-known scholarly treatment of the topic, asserts the following. The interested reader is encouraged to review his numerous sources in further detail.

---

[144] Genesis 1:6-8, 14-15, 17, 20
[145] Victor P. Hamilton, *The Book of Genesis: Chapters 1-17*, (Eerdmans Publishing Co., 1990), 122.

'The basic historical fact that defines the meaning of raqia in Genesis 1 is simply this: *all* peoples in the ancient world thought of the sky as solid. This concept did not begin with the Greeks.

The question, however, arises in the modern mind, schooled as it is in the almost infinite nature of sky and space: Did scientifically naive peoples really believe in a solid sky, or were they just employing a mythological or poetic concept? Or were they, perhaps, just using phenomenal language with no attending belief that the sky actually was a solid object? That is, were they referring to the mere appearance of the sky as a solid dome but able to distinguish between that appearance and the reality?

The answer to these questions, as we shall see more clearly below, is that scientifically naive peoples employed their concept of a solid sky in their mythology, but that they nevertheless thought of the solid sky as an integral part of their physical universe. And it is precisely because ancient peoples were scientifically naive that they did not distinguish between the appearance of the sky and their scientific concept of the sky. They had no reason to doubt what their eyes told them was true, namely, that the stars above them were fixed in a solid dome and that the sky literally touched the earth at the horizon. So, they equated appearance with reality and concluded that the sky must be a solid physical part of the universe just as much as the earth itself.'[146]

Dr. Gregory Beale, Professor of NT and Biblical Theology at Westminster Theological Seminary, diverges from Seely's conclusion.

'There are several points of disagreement that I have with this article, though space does not allow elaboration of all of them. For example, **we just do not know that all ancients believed the sky was a solid dome or that there was anything near unanimity on this point**. The

---

[146] Paul Seely, 'The Firmament and the Water Above Part I: The Meaning of Raqia in Gen. 1:6-8,' *Westminster Theological Journal* 53:2 (1991): 229.

mythological portrayal in the Enuma Elish of the splitting of Tiamat's body does not prove the point from the Babylonian view, despite Seely's protestation to the contrary, since we cannot be sure that the body of the deity would have been thought of as a solid. The deity Apsu is composed of liquid; indeed even Tiamat is the deity of saltwater deep and equated with that reality. Would the Babylonians have thought of saltwater as something solid? Furthermore, the Israelites and other ancient peoples observed that the sun, moon, and planets move across the sky at different rates, which seems to indicate that these were not implanted in a solid-like dome.

Like Seely, Dennis Lamoureux believes that the ANE viewed the heavens as a solid dome-like structure. Lamoureux cites an illustration of the Egyptian view in which the sun god Re travels by boat on the top of a dome shaped sea of the heaven, which is represented by a deity bending over. But there is another Egyptian depiction where the god of the sky, Nut, is held up by Shu, which represents the air itself. Neither the fluid heavenly sea represented by Nut, nor the air symbolized by Shu, are solid materials.

Therefore, rather than considered as a completely solid substance the raqia is perhaps best thought of as diaphanously spread out and transparent. Thus, 'expanse' may be the best translation. The word has this notion in Isaiah 42:5 and 44:24. Even in Exodus 39:3, the verbal form is used for hammering out gold into gold leaf; i.e. **the emphasis does not appear to be so much on the substance but on the spreading out of it**. Thus the focus is on the expansive nature, in that the raqia which Genesis 1:8 defines as 'heaven' is spread out from horizon to horizon. ...

If Seely were correct about the solid nature of the expanse, there would have to be eight solid domes for each light source, evidence of which can be found nowhere in the ancient world. In this respect, biblical writers and ancient astronomers were aware of the five visible light sources – Venus, Mercury, Jupiter, Saturn, Mars – which moved at different rates and sometimes different directions (retrograde motion) from each other and from all the other stars. This might be feasible if each star were embedded in its own separate dome, but not if each is rooted in the same solid dome that houses the other stars. The ancients knew about the moon and sun, which travel at different rates from each other and from all the rest. To accommodate all this complexity of motion would, therefore, require eight domes, each with independent rates of rotation, if the ancients thought of these celestial objects as fixed in a solid firmament. Such a view of multiple domes, however, cannot be found to have existed in the ancient world.'[147]

Dr. Paul Kissling, Professor of OT at TCM Institute describes a fair balance between the conclusions of both Seely and Beale.

'The word translated 'expanse' (עִיקָר, raqia`) comes from a Hebrew verb meaning 'to stamp or spread', sometimes of beating out metal into thin sheets. The word is translated as 'firmament' in the KJV because of the Latin Vulgate firmamentum implying something firm or solid. But the word only occurs eight times outside of this chapter and always elsewhere in poetic context. Ezekiel 1:22 and Daniel 12:3 describe it as shiny or sparkling. Perhaps this suggests that it was viewed as a glass dome covering the earth. But we must remember that these are poetic texts and the language is undoubtedly figurative. Elihu asks Job, 'Can you join him in spreading out the skies hard as a mirror of cast bronze?' (Job 37:18). But again this is poetry and Elihu undoubtedly refers to the mysterious fact that the **invisible skies are strong enough to support the clouds** (37:16). And furthermore the meaning of a related verb in Hebrew cannot by itself tell us what a noun which is derived from it means. Here the firmament is a hyponym of the word 'heaven' or 'sky' (מַיִם shämäyim), that is, it is a synonym for heaven (1:8 God called the expanse 'sky'), **but refers only to one part** of the heavens (1:20 'the expanse of the sky'). The expanse is the space between the water on earth and the water carried in the clouds. In the expanse birds fly and the greater and lesser lights appear. **There is no modern English word which is fully equivalent. Our word atmosphere works in part, but we do not**

[147] Gregory K. Beale, *The Erosion of Inerrancy in Evangelicalism*, (Crossway Books, 2008), 198-199. Emphasis mine.

refer to the sun and moon as being in the atmosphere (1:14). **We must constantly keep in mind that Genesis one is not a scientific treatise, and it uses ordinary language, not scientific language.** We also speak of the sun rising in popular language even though we know that scientifically the sun does not rise at all; the earth turns to face it.'[148]

Dr. Randall Younker, Professor of OT and Biblical Archaeology at Andrews University presents additional evidence that would seem to support the reading of a solid raqia`, *but not the assumed dome like shape.*

'Three basic lines of evidence are presented in defense of this view [the solid dome theory] of ancient Hebrew cosmology: (1) the Hebrews held this view in common with their ancient neighbors, especially Mesopotamia; (2) the Greek (LXX/Septuagint) and Latin (Vulgate) translate the Hebrew raqia‘ of Gen 1:6 as stereōma and firmamentum respectively, showing that raqia‘ means something solid like an inverted metal dome or vault; (3) raqia‘ itself carries the sense of stamped or pounded metal. Because arguments 1 and 2 have impacted argument 3—that is, both the assumption that Israel‘s ancient neighbors held to such an inverted metal bowl cosmology and the Greek and Latin seem to support this have led to how lexicons define the Hebrew raqia‘—it is important to review the evidence for the first two arguments before looking at the meaning of raqia‘ itself.

Biblical scholars already in the nineteenth century began entertaining the idea that the ancients believed in a solid vault of heaven. Then, in 1850, Hormuzd Rassam discovered seven tablets in Ashurbanipal‘s library at Nineveh that were found to contain a Mesopotamian creation account, now known as the Enuma Elish. The original composition may date into the late second millennium, ca. 1100 B.C. during the time of Nebuchadnezzar I. One of the first scholars to utilize this creation account in an attempt to reconstruct an ancient Babylonian cosmology was the German

---

[148] Paul J. Kissling, *Genesis Volume 1*, (College Press Publishing Co., 2004), 102. Emphasis mine.

Assyriologist Peter Jensen in 1890. In Tablets IV and V the basic Babylonian cosmogony and cosmology were outlined. The creation of the Himmelswölbung (heavenly vault) appears on line 145 of tablet IV. Works like Jensen's added support to the pan-Babylonian school led by scholars like Friedrich Delitzsch (1850–1922), who argued that Hebrews received many of their ideas about primeval history, including their creation story, from the Babylonians during the exile. Soon, a number of critical scholars augmented the Hebrew meaning of raqia' in lexicons, commentaries, etc. by adding the idea of a solid vault, usually composed of metal.

Then, in 1975, when Assyriologist W. G. Lambert tried to locate the idea that the Babylonians conceived of the firmament as a solid vault in original Babylonian sources, his search came up empty! The closest support he could find was Jensen's original 1890 study which translated the Babylonian word for heaven in Enuma Elish IV 145 as Himmelswölbung or vault of heaven. Although Lambert generally admires Jensen's pioneering work, he notes that Jensen made this translation without any support or justification whatsoever. Rather, Jensen simply makes the translation and then proceeds thereafter as if the point is proved. Apparently Jensen accepted the common assumption that the Babylonians conceived of the firmament in this way and arbitrarily translated the Babylonian word for heaven as a vault! However, after reviewing the evidence, Lambert concluded, **The idea of a vault of heaven [in ancient Babylonian literature] is not based on any piece of evidence**. Rather, Lambert notes that **the ancient Babylonians viewed the cosmos as a series of flat, superimposed layers of the same size separated by space, held together by ropes; there was no hint of a solid dome.**

Lambert's study was taken up by his student, Wayne Horowitz, who notes that although the clear sky seems to us to be shaped like a dome, rather than a flat circle, there is no direct evidence that ancient Mesopotamians thought the visible heavens to be a dome. Akkadian kippatu are always flat, circular objects such as geometric circles or hoops, rather than three dimensional domes. **The fact remains that there is no word for a heavenly domed vault in ancient Mesopotamia.'**[149]

Surprisingly, though, it appears Dr. Younker was not aware of Dr. Lambert's specific view of the raqia` in Genesis 1.

> 'On the second day the cosmic water is separated into upper and lower parts, **by a 'vault'**. The Hebrew word means something beaten out, like a metal plate, and the AV's 'firmament' is unhelpful. **This plate serves to hold back the upper water and is called 'heaven'.**'[150]

Thomas Aquinas clearly outlines at least two different opinions on the nature of the raqia`, extant in the 13th century. One of these was a solid atmosphere, and the other was the location of the stars beyond the solid atmosphere.

> 'In discussing questions of this kind two rules are to be observed, as Augustine teaches (Gen. ad lit. i, 18). The first is, to hold the truth of Scripture without wavering. The second is that **since Holy Scripture can be explained in a multiplicity of senses, one should adhere to a particular explanation, only in such measure as to be ready to abandon it, if it be proved with certainty to be false**; lest Holy Scripture be exposed to the ridicule of unbelievers, and obstacles be placed to their believing.
>
> We say, therefore, that the words which speak of the firmament as made on the second day **can be understood in two senses**. They may be understood, **first, of the starry firmament**, on which point it is necessary to set forth the different opinions of philosophers. Some of these believed it to be composed of the elements; and this was the opinion of Empedocles, who, however, held further that the body of the firmament was not susceptible of dissolution, because its parts are, so to say, not in disunion, but in harmony. Others held the firmament to be of the nature of the four

---

[149] Randall Younker, 'Crucial Questions of Interpretation in Genesis 1', 1 Oct 2009, <https://adventistbiblicalresearch.org/sites/default/files/pdf/Crucial%20Questions%20of%20Interpretation%20in%20Genesis%201.pdf> (10 Mar 2015). Emphasis mine.

[150] Wilfred Lambert, 'Creation', *Endeavour Magazine* 96 (1996): 30.

elements, not, indeed, compounded of them, but being as it were a simple element. Such was the opinion of Plato, who held that element to be fire. Others, again, have held that the heaven is not of the nature of the four elements, but is itself a fifth body, existing over and above these. This is the opinion of Aristotle (De Coel. i, text. 6,32). …

Another possible explanation is to understand by the firmament that was made on the second day, not that in which the stars are set, but **the part of the atmosphere where the clouds are collected, and which has received the name firmament from the firmness and density of the air. "For a body is called firm," that is dense and solid**, "thereby differing from a mathematical body" as is remarked by Basil (Hom. iii in Hexaem.). If, then, this explanation is adopted none of these opinions will be found repugnant to reason. Augustine, in fact (Gen. ad lit. ii, 4), recommends it thus: "I consider this view of the question worthy of all commendation, as neither contrary to faith nor difficult to be proved and believed.'[151]

The noted science historian Dr. Edward Grant provides extraordinary insight into this difficult and fascinating question.

'A widely held opinion today is that scholastic authors thought the celestial orbs were solid, where "solid" is taken as synonymous with hard or rigid. Here the image is one of transparent glass or crystalline globes. Hardly in contention as to popularity with the first opinion today is a second, which assumes that medieval thinkers faithfully adhered to Aristotle's dicta about the celestial ether. **Thus the orbs or spheres could be neither solid nor fluid** because Aristotle had argued that contrary qualities such as hardness and softness, density and rarity, and so on, were inapplicable to the incorruptible, celestial ether of which they were composted. Nicholas Jardine observes (1982, 175) that **to pose a question about the hardness or softness of celestial spheres**

---

[151] Fathers of the English Dominican Province, trans., *Summa Theologica, Pt. 1: Q68*, <http://www.ccel.org/ccel/aquinas/summa/FP/FP068.html#FPQ68OUTP1>. Emphasis mine.

would have been considered a 'category mistake.'
Hardness and softness are qualitative opposites found
only in terrestrial matter. Since pairs of opposite qualities
are the source of all terrestrial change, they must of
necessity be absent from celestial region, where change
is impossible. Thus to inquire about the possible
hardness or softness of celestial orbs is to ask an
irrelevant question. ...

Indeed, the debate hinged on the interpretation placed on
the terms 'waters' (aquae) and 'firmament'
(firmamentum), the latter largely determining the
meaning of the former...
From the time of the Church Fathers to the end of the
Middle Ages, **a variety of interpretations of the waters
above the firmament were proposed**. The interpreters
divide essentially into two groups: those who thought of
the waters as solid and hard and those who considered
them fluid. Among the former we may include Saint
Jerome and Bede...Those who assumed that the waters
above the firmament were fluid formed the larger group
during the Middle Ages and included Ambrose, John
Damascene, Alexander of Hales, Robert Grosseteste,
Richard of Middleton, Saint Bonaventure, Vincent of
Beauvais, and an anonymous author of a French
encyclopedia written around 1400...

For many, if not most, of those who considered the
suprafirmamental waters 'crystalline', the latter term did
not signify the hardness of the waters but rather their
immutability, transparency and luminosity. When
medieval authors spoke of the crystalline sphere, they
usually had in mind those properties of a crystal such as
luminosity, transparency, and even a quasi immutability,
rather than hardness. ...

The hypothesis of fluid heavens, which went largely
unchallenged prior to the thirteenth century, came to
have a rival after the introduction and dissemination of
Aristolean-Ptolemaic astronomy and cosmology in the
thirteenth century. **Whereas previously the idea of a
fluid or soft heavens was overwhelmingly dominant,
the existence of orbs and their possible hardness now
emerged as an opposition hypothesis.'**[152]

Dr. Walton may summarize the issue in the best way possible.

'Everyone in the ancient world believed there were waters above (since it sometimes came down) and waters below (since you could dig to find water and since there were springs where the waters emerged). No new scientific information is being given here; the text reflects the ways in which everyone in the ancient world thought about the cosmos and has particular significance for what they believed about the weather. God accomplished this separation by means of the raqia` (vault, expanse, firmament). Prior to the midsecond millennium A.D., this term was consistently understood as a solid sky that held back the rain. When it became widely recognized that the sky was not solid, other translations began to be used that focused more on the lower levels of the atmosphere, using non technical terms such as expanse or vault.

Everyone in the ancient world believed in a solid sky, **although there were varying opinions about its composition.** The Israelites undoubtedly believed in a solid sky, although it is open to question whether raqia` is the word for that solid sky. For many years, I believed that it was. Further reflection and more recent research, however, have led me to a different conclusion as I have encountered another Hebrew word that I believe refers to the solid sky. If this is the case, raqia` instead refers to the space created by the separating of the waters that are held back by the solid sky. That space would be the living space for all creatures. This space is significant in Ancient Near Eastern cosmologies, particularly in Egypt, where they associate it with the god Shu. Ancient cosmology is reflected in the Hebrew Bible since **the sun and moon are together in this space.** But most important for our discussion, we recognize again that we are not being introduced to the manufacture of a material object. In Israelite perception, **the space is not material. (We cannot bring in the concept of molecules of hydrogen and oxygen; that is no longer thinking with the text.)**[153]

---

[152] Edward Grant, *Planets, Stars, and Orbs: The Medieval Cosmos, 1200-1687*, (Cambridge University Press, 1996), 324-325, 334, 338.

After all this, we must question those who would insist upon a modern, literal interpretation of Genesis 1. Was the raqia` solid, liquid, or something else? Was it a dome, or was it a flat disk? Was it single layered, or multi layered? Was it made of metal, or crystal, or some other type of matter? Was it merely a phenomenological expression? All of these questions are, for the modern Bible student, spiritually irrelevant. This does not mean we cannot investigate these questions, for the purpose of our own curiosity, but at the same time we cannot possibly impose upon other believers a singular set of answers.

The large body of evidence amassed by Seely proves the universal acceptance of the ancient solid sky, but does not by extension automatically prove that raqia` was the appropriate word for it. While we might prefer to reduce the raqia` to a space 'spread out' between the waters, as Dr. Beale suggests, this is a bit of an oversimplification. It does nothing to ease the modern literal predicament. This space must still reside below a global body of water in the sky, according to the plain literal reading, which even Dr. Beale admits. For ancient Israel, the assumed solid sky was either the top layer of the raqia`[154], or above the raqia` entirely.[155] Dr. Walton believes this physical structure is best described by a different Hebrew word found in Job 37:18, 21.[156]

---

[153] John Walton, *The Lost World of Adam and Eve*, (InterVarsity Press, 2015), 35-36. Emphasis mine.
[154] 'Ben Zoma concluded that there is 'only a bare three fingers breadth' between the waters above and the waters below; *cf. b. Hag.* 15a(92); see also *Gen. R.* 2,4 where the figure given is 'two or three fingerbreadths' and *j. Hag.* 2, 77a-b where the measurement is 'about a wide handsbreadth'. **Different opinions about the thickness of the firmament are expressed** in *Gen. R.* 4,5 and *b. Pesah* 94a (502-503). Emphasis mine. See Michael Maher, *Targum Pseudo Jonathan: Genesis*, (The Liturgical Press, 1992), 17.
[155] For a thorough review of the variety of Classical Age rabbinical opinions on the raqia' see Moshe Simon-Shoshan, 'The Heavens Proclaim the Glory of God – A Study in Rabbinic Cosmology' *B.D.D.*, 2008: 67-96. <https://www.academia.edu/688606/A_Study_in_Rabbinic_Cosmology>
[156] John Walton, *Genesis 1 As Ancient Cosmology*, (Eisenbrauns, 2011), 155-161.

Indeed, Thomas Aquinas verifies that the raqia` did *not* represent all of the celestial arena, but rather that there was confusion in the Medieval Age as to *what portion* of the celestial arena the raqia` actually referred to. Dr. Kissling's comments are particularly interesting, because he indicates that it is impossible to precisely describe in English the original meaning of raqia`. Dr. Grant verifies for us the contrasting opinions in the late Classical and early Medieval Ages, with the majority in favor of either fluid or non-material, before indicating the popular swing back towards the solid view in the late Medieval Age.

So then it is true that Ancient, Classical, and Medieval peoples all maintained contradictory opinions as to the specific physical composition of the raqia`. For those defending a solid view of the raqia`, there are sources available. For those defending a non-solid view, opposing sources can be found as well. This is only because both views have been held, with differing majorities at different times in history. We can't even agree on what exactly we are talking about, let alone agree on what it is made out of. This is an inherently modern mistake!

The ancient belief in the 'solid sky' is indisputable irrespective of, as Dr. Walton puts it, the 'varying opinions about its composition'. **This distinction is critical.** The space between the waters performed two very important, ancient functions. These functions are unequivocal, regardless of how they were presumed to be implemented. Disagreements over the specific shape, composition or location of the raqia` do nothing to undermine the universal acceptance of these functions.

In the first place, God created a celestial support structure for a global body of physical waters above, as we have seen. But beyond that, God also created something else using the raqia` which was much more important. Dr. Smith brings to our attention this second aspect which is so very often ignored by modern literal expositors. 'The word raqia` in Gen. 1:6-7, often translated 'firmament', stands in parallelism with 'the heavens' in Psalm 19:1 (MT 2). In Psalm 150:1, the same word is parallel to 'His holy place' and in apposition to 'His strong place'. From these comparisons, the firmament is located **in the heavens**, and **it is the site of Divine enthronement in the heavens**.'[157]

Dr. Paula Gooding, visiting lecturer at Kings College London, concurs.

'Although modern science has overturned a view of the world in which the blue sky is seen as holding back the waters above, **intimations of this view of the world linger on in phrases like 'the heavens opened'.** In Hebrew cosmology, rains was understood as occurring on those occasions when the windows of heaven were opened and the waters were being held back came through to fall on the earth once more. ... We are left, then, with the question of how the raqia` relates to heaven (the Hebrew word shamayim). ... In the book of Ezekiel it is used five times to describe not the created order but the design of God's chariot (Ez. 1:22, 23, 25, 26: 10:1).

This second usage in Ezekiel helps us to understand something important about the raqia`. Here the raqia` was spread over the head of the winged living creatures, and provided a platform upon which God's throne rested. The chariot, then, seems to mimic the design of the world as a whole: **just as God's throne rested on the raqia` of the chariot, so too did it rest on the raqia` of the created world. It becomes clear then that the raqia` serves not just as the barrier for water but as the place upon which God's throne could rest.** This is further illustrated in Exodus 24 when Moses, Aaron, Nadab, Abihu, and 70 of the elders of Israel saw God on the top of Mt. Sinai and under His feet 'there was something like a pavement of sapphire stone, like the very heaven for clearness' (Exod. 24:10). Here again we have a tradition that beneath God was something like the raqia`, even when He was not in heaven. This became an important strand in later reflections on the throne of God, being picked up again both in Revelation 4:6, 'and in front of the throne there is something like a sea of glass, like crystal', and in later, more elaborate texts which reflect in more depth on the nature of the throne of God.'[158]

---

[157] Mark Smith, *The Priestly Vision of Genesis 1*, (Fortress Press, 2010), 201. Emphasis mine.
[158] Paula Gooding, *Heaven*, (Cascade Books, 2011), 4-5. Emphasis mine.

The raqia` therefore, as the place of God's throne, is truly the straw that breaks the modern literal expositor's back. 'Thus says the LORD:
'**Heaven is my throne**, and the earth is my footstool'[159], and again 'Do not take an oath at all, **either by heaven, for it is the throne of God**, or by the earth, for it is his footstool.'[160] '**Yet the Most High does not dwell in houses made by hands**, as the prophet says, '**Heaven is my throne**, and the earth is my footstool. What kind of house will you build for me, says the Lord, or what is the place of my rest?'[161] Such a predicament illustrates exactly why the plain, literal meaning of raqia` does not apply to us today.

The fact that no modern Christian actually imagines that God physically sits on a Divine throne, at a specific point in space, is irrelevant. All ANE cultures, including the Jewish culture, did believe that the raqia` below the waters above was a physical place for deity. This idea no longer exists, in its ancient conceptual form. In fact, it *never* literally existed in its ancient conceptual form. The text cannot be construed therefore to communicate such principles for us in their plain, literal sense.

Often, Bible students are more than content to concede this point in part. They admit that God does not literally sit on top of heaven, as if it were a Divine throne, nor does He even possess feet with which He may refer to the literal earth as His 'footstool'. However, many of these same Bible students completely ignore the undeniable result of their interpretive conclusion. In order for God to sit as it were on a throne, said throne **must** have sufficient physical rigidity and strength to support Him! If it does not, the entire word picture is destroyed. We cannot reinterpret the plain, literal reading of Scripture which tells us that God physically sits on a throne, while at the same time clinging tightly to the modern, literal existence of this tangible throne, *which is the raqia`*.

Some would dispute this conclusion, for example, on the basis that the word raqia` is not found in Isaiah 66:1. The heaven which is

---

[159] Isaiah 66:1
[160] Matthew 5:34-35
[161] Acts 7:48-49

defined as God's throne is there referred to as shamayim, rather than raqia`. But let us examine the evidence even further.

First, the concept of 'heaven' and 'earth', as two halves of a whole creation, is termed a merism. Two or more components of a larger assembly are often used as shorthand to refer to the larger assembly. This is what we find in Genesis 1:1, for example. The 'heaven' actually refers to the whole upper half of creation, including birds, sun, moon, stars, the waters above the raqia`, and of course the raqia` itself. Similarly, the 'earth' actually refers to the whole lower half of creation, including the animals, plants, and humans. This does not override the fact that, in other instances, those same two terms may still refer only to the specific portion of creation to which they were assigned. The principal component of 'heaven' is still the raqia`, and the principal component of 'earth' is still the dry land.

Second, Isaiah specifically states that human attempts to construct a temple or 'house' for God simply fall short when we realize that the whole of creation, the 'heaven' and the 'earth', is God's temple. 'All these things my hand has made, and so all these things came to be declares the Lord'.[162] This is a deliberate comparison with a physical object, for a spiritual purpose. Isaiah's words echo those of King Solomon, at the dedication ceremony of Israel's first temple.[163] But what type of comparison is being made? It is obviously a comparison between two *structures*. A human structure is compared with a Divine structure.

So then, while Isaiah's scope of reference to creation is clearly universal, it still requires a structural component within both the lower and upper halves of that creation. Without them the literary comparison between structures would immediately collapse. The fact that the passage reads naturally as a merism makes no difference. Of course, God rules over everything He has created, but without the raqia` there is nothing to sit on, and without the dry land there is nowhere to put His feet. This is precisely why the raqia` was chosen and named, out of all the components of the upper half of creation, to represent the rest as the shamayim or 'heaven'.

---

[162] Isaiah 66:2
[163] I Kings 8:27; II Chronicles 6:18

The Psalms go on to teach us that God's throne is 'in heaven'. [164] So to be 'in heaven' is to be part of heaven in a generic sense. The throne of God is in the upper half of His creation, which means the throne itself is just one portion of it. Again, this is sensible, because the word picture requires a structural raqia`. There is no other component of the 'heaven' that was thought to function like a chair.

Perhaps, though, Ezekiel's vision of a raqia` has also introduced some uncertainty. Is the raqia` the throne itself, specifically, or is the raqia` merely underneath the throne? If we have asked this question, then we have missed the point entirely. In the first place, Ezekiel's image is only 'a' raqia`. It is not necessarily the same raqia`, as that found in Genesis 1, and the text does not intend to convey otherwise. Ezekiel only identifies it by way of similarity. In the second place, the question is spiritually irrelevant. Our purpose is not to reconcile, in piecemeal fashion, all the Biblical references to God's throne in the Bible as if we could reconstruct a complete physical picture. The throne is not a physical reality. We are not actually talking about a fixed object in outer space. This is merely spiritual imagery based on literal concepts. So very often in Scripture, a spiritual image is presented in one way to make a particular point in one place, and in another way in another place to make a different point. It is enough here to demonstrate that when the word raqia` is used, it is always with respect to tangible structure.

We may not understand this, or know how to apply it yet, but our understanding cannot progress if it is not first based on sound reason. Although the word raqia` is physical in nature, it nevertheless conveys a spiritual reality, and we cannot always force the spiritual to conform to the physical. For example, it is perfectly acceptable for Isaiah to refer to the whole of 'heaven' as God's throne, and he does not contradict David who says that God's throne is 'in heaven'. The lesson for us is merely that spiritual imagery requires grammar which actually contributes to the point being made.

---

[164] Psalm 11:4, 103:19

To be fair, the study of grammar alone can never solve all our exegetical problems. So then we have examined the etymology of the word raqia', as well as its general use case, and even its spiritual use case. And these examinations agree. The word raqia' conveys a tangible structure which, according to ancient Israel, both served as a barrier for liquid water as well as a place for God to sit. At the same time, the word raqia' alone does not convey any particular shape, composition, or location.

Today, the word raqia' is often translated in a seemingly anonymous sense as 'expanse'. But we have shown that this is only a rough and incomplete approximation. Without extraordinary evidence, we cannot arbitrarily reduce a Hebrew word with inherent structural function to an English word that carries no inherent structural function. The fact is that the original, ancient concept of raqia' does not exist for us today. It was not anything which we can describe in modern terms. It was not just the space between the waters, or our modern atmosphere.

In the end, the only honest literal view of Genesis 1 is that of the ancient Jewish people. It is the only variant which does not require grammatical abuse of the text. It is the only variant which is in harmony with the popular understanding of natural mechanics at the time the text was written. Forcing wild and unsubstantiated ideas upon the passage after the fact, to explain away the obvious, literal conflicts of the ancient reading only serves to prove the point. To the ancient reader, there are no literal conflicts with the natural world in Genesis 1. Everything is as it appears to the common observer, apart from the influence of science. There is nothing to explain away. The literal conflicts are ours, not theirs.

Is it truly rational then to demand that the Bible student accept a modern mechanical reading of Genesis 1? How much of the text must we believe, in the plain sense, and with what latitude may we amend the plain sense? What remains as an uncertain detail? How many Bible students are simply unaware that these and *many* other details have been the focus of so many disputes? Forcing the text into any modern framework contradicts reason, creates innumerable problems, promotes controversy, and repeats the mistakes of history. We must understand why the language of Genesis 1 made sense to the ancient mind, and why it often does *not* mean what the modern reader might simply assume. We are not allowed to force additional modern meaning, to avoid conflict, as if we had the supreme authority to redefine a dead language and culture after the fact.

III. 7000 Years Of Creation?

Many Jews and Christians, from the 2nd century BCE to the 18th century, believed that the days of creation symbolically represented details of world events, or ages, in 1,000 year increments. This popular theory was both quite poetic and superficially plausible. It appeared to be a very convenient way in which God's Word could be utilized to predict the future. However, this is no longer the case, and for good reasons.

Much evidence for the aforementioned 7000 year creation theory can be found in Appendix I. Incidentally, this theory also led to the related view that the age of the physical earth itself could not exceed 7000 years. Although both of these ideas lost much of their popularity by the end of the Pre-Modern Age, they were allowed to persist essentially unchallenged up until that point. They have even seen some resurgence amongst fundamentalist groups today.

Ellen White, who helped found the Seventh Day Adventist denomination in the mid 19th century, was very instrumental in reviving the 7,000 year creation theory in a series of self-proclaimed visions which were accepted as of Divine origin by her followers.[165] George McCready Price was an avid supporter of Ellen White, and gave White's ancient ideas a wider audience in several geology books in the late 19th and early 20th centuries.[166] Finally, in 1961,

---

[165] '**For six thousand years** the great controversy has been in progress; the Son of God and His heavenly messengers have been in conflict with the power of the evil one, to warn, enlighten, and save the children of men.' Emphasis mine. See Ellen White, 'Great Controversy', <http://www.whiteestate.org/books/gc/gc41.html>.

[166] White's interpretation of the biblical narratives attracted little interest outside Adventist circles, but within the Adventist tradition her writings acquired a stature comparable to scripture. Her interpretation of the Flood became widely known outside Adventist circles through the writings of George McCready Price (1870-1963). A self-taught geologist with limited education beyond high school, Price was a gifted writer, amateur scientist, and tireless crusader in the cause of anti-evolution. His 723-page *The New*

Henry Morris and John Whitcomb published 'The Genesis Flood' in which they borrowed heavily from Price's work and sparked significant controversy by catapulting a young earth perspective back into the evangelical spotlight.[167]

But herein lies the root problem. Symbolic timeline calculations fall at the mercy of a very persistent enemy, which is the passage of time itself. In fact, by the time the Seventh Day Adventist views on creation hit the headlines, mainstream evangelical organizations had long given up on the 7,000 year creation theory.[168, 169] If not for the supernatural visions of Ellen White, so called, we might now only be able to read about this particular view in history books. And yet, it is persistently claimed by some that this calculated 7000 year timeline does indeed derive from Biblical sources. So we must examine the evidence.

The 7,000 year theory is first attributed by the Talmud to OT passages such as Psalm 90:4, Isaiah 2:2, and Hosea 6:1. However, it is well known that the rabbis had a reputation for heavy embellishment of the Biblical text. In this case, the Biblical texts do not clearly state what the rabbis assumed. For example, in Psalm 90:4, it merely states that what appears to be a long time in human terms, that is a thousand years, is actually only a short time from God's perspective. The verse is, in grammatical terms, a simile.

Geology, published in 1923, was catapulted into relevance by William Jennings Bryan, who prosecuted John Scopes at the famous trial in Dayton, Tennessee, in 1925. **But even Bryan, the most important anti-evolutionist of the first half of the 20th century was not a young-earth creationist**, seeing no reason to interpret the Genesis creation account as taking place over a literal seven-day week. Emphasis mine. See Karl Giberson, *Adventist Origins of Young Earth Creationism*, <http://biologos.org/uploads/static-content/Giberson-scholarly-essay-1.pdf>.

[167] Wikipedia contributors. "The Genesis Flood." Wikipedia, The Free Encyclopedia. Wikipedia, The Free Encyclopedia, 5 Nov. 2014. Web. 7 Jun. 2015.

[168] Wikipedia contributors. "American Scientific Affiliation." Wikipedia, The Free Encyclopedia. Wikipedia, The Free Encyclopedia, 30 May. 2015. Web. 7 Jun. 2015.

[169] Wikipedia contributors. "Christians in Science." Wikipedia, The Free Encyclopedia. Wikipedia, The Free Encyclopedia, 24 May. 2015. Web. 7 Jun. 2015.

Numerous other examples of this literary technique can be illustrated throughout the Bible, which do not require a direct symbolic replacement of the latter with the former. Unfortunately, early Christians who also proposed a 1,000 year period for each day of creation merely copied this inference from the Jewish sources before them.

But why? The answer requires an examination of the underlying Jewish motivation. The Jews who first documented the concept of the calculated creation timeline were struggling to make sense of the sad state of Jewish affairs, and desperate in their anticipation of the coming Messiah. They were of the same class of whom Isaiah refers to with the words, 'keep on hearing, but do not understand; keep on seeing, but do not perceive.'[170] While this does not give us license to reject their entire testimony out of hand, nevertheless we as modern Christians must simply keep in mind the context of our sources. We must take the Jewish ideas presented to us with a grain of salt accordingly.

Certainly, it is not reasonable to think that the Jews, who ultimately rejected Christ, had in any way succeeded in unlocking God's creation mystery. If the 7,000 year theory was correct, it would represent a fundamental breakthrough in their spiritual understanding, and further it would produce testable predictions. But the calculated creation timeline failed on both counts, and it is important to understand why these failures occurred. To that end, it is helpful to take a bird's eye view of the historical wreckage.

Numerous attempts were made by expositors throughout history to calculate the age of the earth based on Bible chronologies, in order to verify the 7,000 year creation theory. And these attempts included both Jews and Christians.

The 17th century Archbishop Ussher published one of the most famous and detailed creation chronologies, based on the Masoretic Text, but he was certainly not alone in this effort. He used Biblical genealogical data in an attempt to confirm the popular theory.

---

[170] Isaiah 6:9

'Most everyone has heard of James Usher (1581-1656), Anglican Archbishop of Armagh in Northern Ireland, and Primate of all Ireland. His precise dating of the moment of the Creation as occurring at nightfall preceding Sunday, Oct. 23, 4004 B.C., is included in the margins of fundamentalist Bibles. Published posthumously in 1658, *Annals of the World* is an extraordinary work attempting to give an account of major events in history from 4004 to 1922 B.C., and from then an almost year by year account up until 73 A.D. It was an attempt to trace back the genealogies in the Bible in literal terms and interweave this with Greek and Roman history. It worked out that the creation had taken place exactly 4,000 years before the birth of Christ, and Ussher also believed that the earth would come to an end exactly 6,000 years after it had been created. Ussher's was not the first nor the last attempt to determine the age of the earth from the Bible. Estimates had been made by the Venerable Bede in 723 (3952 BC) and John Lightfoot in 1644 (3929 BC), and later by Johannes Kepler (3992 BC), and Isaac Newton (4000 BC) among others.'[171]

Dr. Floyd Jones notes another, more extensive list of Pre-Modern expositors who attempted to calculate the date of creation.

'The date of Creation as taken from the Scriptures has been calculated by many scholars over the centuries resulting in a significant divergence of solutions. As is true for nearly each of the natural major time segments into which Biblical chronology has been divided (i.e. the 430 year sojourn, the 480 years from Exodus to the commencement of the Temple etc.), the answers fall into two general categories, that of the 'Long Chronology' or the 'Short Chronology'.

---

[171] William Hay, *Experimenting on A Small Planet: A Scholarly Entertainment*, (Springer, 2012), 63.

Chronologist	When Calculated?	Date B.C.
John Jackson	1752	5426
Dr William Hales	c. 1830	5411
Thomas Lydiat	c. 1600	4103
M. Michael Maestlinus	c. 1600	4079
Jacob Salianus	c. 1600	4053
H. Spondanus	c. 1600	4051
J. Cappellus	c. 1600	4005
E. Greswell	1830	4004
D. Petavius	c. 1627	3983
C. Longomontanus	c. 1600	3966
P. Melanchthon	c. 1550	3964
A. Salmeron	d. 1585	3958
J. Scaliger	d. 1609	3949
M. Beroaldus	c. 1575	3927
A. Helwigius	c. 1630	3836

Table 14: Calculated Dates Of Creation

The preceding table portrays the calculated interval from the Creation to the birth of Christ Jesus and depicts an objective sampling of chronologers over the past several hundred years…

The scatter effect may seem strange and unaccountable to many, but by now most probably already begin to see some of the rationale leading up to the unevenness in the results. John Jackson and Dr. William Hales are representative of those who used the Septuagint for the patriarchal generations and other 'Long' interval determinations (as that with the Exodus, see discussion on Chart 3). The 'Short Chronology' is the result of relying upon the Hebrew; the disagreements are the result of differing opinions and interpretations by the individual workers within the Masoretic Text and of some coming to the task with various doctrinal presuppositions to maintain.'[172]

Dr. Jones shows us what many other historians and scholars have similarly noted. The significant genealogical conflicts between the Septuagint and Masoretic Texts are, in a nutshell, the primary reason for the so called 'long' and 'short' chronologies. 'Many of the earliest Christians who followed the Septuagint calculated creation around 5500 BC, and Christians up to the Middle-Ages continued to use this rough estimate: Clement of Alexandria (5592 BC),Theophilus of Antioch (5529 BC), Julius Africanus (5501 BC), Hippolytus of Rome (5500 BC), Gregory of Tours (5500 BC), Panodorus of Alexandria (5493 BC), Maximus the Confessor (5493 BC), George Syncellus (5492 BC) Sulpicius Severus (5469 BC), Isidore of Seville (5336 BC), Eusebius (5228 BC), and Jerome (5199 BC). The Byzantine calendar has traditionally dated the creation of the world to September 1, 5509 BC.'[173] Not surprisingly, the Jewish historian Josephus came to a similar conclusion in the 1st century, when majority emphasis was placed on the Septuagint. [174]

---

[172] Floyd Jones, *Chronology of the Old Testament: A Return to the Basics*, (KingsWord Press, 2002) 26-27.

[173] Wikipedia contributors. "Dating creation." *Wikipedia, The Free Encyclopedia*. Wikipedia, The Free Encyclopedia, 16 Mar. 2015. Web. 22 Mar. 2015.

[174] In his monumental Antiquities of the Jews, Josephus dictates a length of time for each of the headings in his twenty part historical chronology. Summing all of these periods together ascribes 5,782 years 'from the original creation of man until the 12th year of the reign of Nero.' See William Whiston trans., *Josephus: The Complete Works*, (Thomas Nelson

To complicate matters even further, a third prominent OT manuscript known as the Samaritan Pentateuch supports a calculated creation date of ~4300 BC, somewhere between the aforementioned 'long' and 'short' chronologies.[175]

When it became clear to the misguided and scattered Jews of the 2nd century that their Messiah had not yet come, Rabbi Jose ben Halafta conveniently proposed an amended date of creation using several, innovative methods of interpretation on the Hebrew texts. 'Adhering closely to the Pharisaic interpretations of Bible texts, he endeavored not only to elucidate many passages, but also to determine certain dates which are not indicated in the Bible, but which may be inferred by calculation. ... In many cases, however, he gave the dates according to tradition, and inserted, besides, the sayings and halakot of preceding rabbis and of his contemporaries. In discussing Biblical chronology he followed three principles:

- To assume that the intention of the Biblical author was, wherever possible, to give exact dates
- To assign to each of a series of events the shortest possible duration of time, where necessary, in order to secure agreement with the Biblical text
- To adopt the lesser of two possible numbers.

The application of these principles would obviously have had the effect of compressing the Biblical chronology.'[176] Ultimately, his desperate assertion that the creation took place in 3761 B.C. would have postponed the presumed deadline of the 4th millennium and extended the hopes of the orthodox community for their Messiah until the mid 3rd century. The Messiah did not come for the Jewish believers in the 3rd century either, and all that remained was to push the anticipated advent of the Messiah to a subsequent millennium.

Publishers, 1998), 650.
[175] Curt Sewell, 'Biblical Chronology And Dating Of The Early Bible', <http://www.ldolphin.org/sewell/sewellchron.html>, 8 Aug 2015.

[176] Wikipedia contributors. 'Seder Olam Rabbah.' *Wikipedia, The Free Encyclopedia.* Wikipedia, The Free Encyclopedia, 3 Aug. 2014. Web. 7 Dec. 2014. Emphasis mine.

'Despite the computations by Jose ben Halafta, confusion persisted for a long time as to how the calculations should be applied. During 1000, for example, the Muslim chronologist al-Biruni noted that three different epochs were used by various Jewish communities being one, two, or three years later than the modern epoch. The epoch seems to have been settled by 1178, when Maimonides, in his work *Mishneh Torah*, described all of the modern rules of the Hebrew calendar, including the modern epochal year. His work has been accepted by Jews as definitive, though it does not correspond to the scientific calculations.'[177] In fact, the modern orthodox Jewish calendar is still based off these calculations, and therefore some Jewish believers anticipate even today that the Messiah must come no later than 2239 C.E., being the end of the supposed 6th millennium.[178]

Both Catholic and Protestant scholars also tried their hand at the calculated creation timeline, but they fared no better. Much of the blame for this can be placed at the feet of Augustine, one of the most revered Church fathers who lived and wrote in the 4th and 5th centuries. Although numerous other expositors had calculated a similar age of the earth, it was Augustine who took great pains to spell out in detail his views on the meaning of the symbolic model. In asserting that Christ had come in the mid 5th millennium, he thus boldly placed himself near the beginning of the 6th millennium of world history. Nearly all Christian expositors after him followed his lead, and so they all proved utterly mistaken approximately one thousand years later, when it became clear that Christ had not yet returned a second time.

'Bede was one of the first to break away from the standard Septuagint date for the creation and in his work De Temporibus ("On Time") (completed in 703 AD) dated the creation to 18 March 3952 BC but was accused of heresy at the table of Bishop Wilfrid, because his chronology was contrary to accepted calculations of around 5500 BC. After the Masoretic text was published, however, dating creation around 4000 BC became common, and was received with wide support.'[179]

---

[177] Ibid.
[178] Wikipedia contributors. 'Year 6000.' *Wikipedia, The Free Encyclopedia*. Wikipedia, The Free Encyclopedia, 25 Sep. 2014. Web. 30 Nov. 2014.

It was certainly no coincidence therefore that the late 16th and early 17th centuries produced dramatic upheaval throughout Christendom. Among many other issues, Biblical scholars were forced to reevaluate Augustine's 7000 year creation symbolism, including the perceived age of the earth. His timeline was quite past due! They found solace in the Masoretic text, and thus there was a sharp rise in the number of late Medieval and Pre Modern age expositors who re-calculated later dates for the origin of the creation so as not to destroy the most popular theory. Christ, who had long been presumed by Christians to have arrived in the 5th millennium, was now quietly pushed back to the 4th.

But even the Masoretic text alone could not save the 7,000 year theory. 'Proposed calculations of the date of creation, using the Masoretic from the 10th century – 18th century include: Marianus Scotus (4192 BC), Maimonides (4058 BC) ... Benedict Pereira (4021 BC), Louis Cappel (4005 BC) ... Augustin Calmet (4002 BC) ... Theodore Bibliander (3980 BC) ... Martin Luther (3961 BC) ... Cornelius Cornelii a Lapide (3951 BC) ... Christoph Helvig (3947 BC), Gerardus Mercator (3928 BC), Matthieu Brouard (3927 BC), Benito Arias Montano (3849 BC) ... David Gans (3761 BC) and Gershom ben Judah (3754 BC).'[180] These dates cover such a wide spectrum, so as to plainly inform us that not one version of the OT has sufficient detail upon which to accurately calculate the alleged 7,000 year theory with any certainty.

So then, all hope for a verifiable Bible calculation has literally been lost in translation.

Does God truly intend that we understand and believe this particular theory? He certainly has made no effort to that end; we simply lack both a clear statement of fact and a mathematical calculation! It is logically impossible for us today to derive said chronology, and this

[179] Wikipedia contributors. "Dating creation." *Wikipedia, The Free Encyclopedia.* Wikipedia, The Free Encyclopedia, 16 Mar. 2015. Web. 22 Mar. 2015.
[180] Wikipedia contributors. "Young Earth creationism." Wikipedia, The Free Encyclopedia. Wikipedia, The Free Encyclopedia, 16 Jul. 2015. Web. 8 Aug. 2015.

should be a strong warning for the modern Bible student. We should not continue to change the rules and invent new methods every time the calculations expire, no matter which text we choose to base our assumptions upon.

Instead, we should learn the lesson here that history has to teach us.

Let us be clear. All of the evidence indicates that something monumental is lurking beneath the spiritual surface of Genesis 1, and this even Israel could perceive. Nevertheless, based on Isaiah's teaching, we know that Israel, as a nation, was spiritually blind and her belief in the original, calculated creation timeline added nothing of value. While the rabbinical tradition did help fuel the Messianic expectations of the 1st century, its apparent connection to reality was only incidental. The general population was not accurately aware of any hidden meaning at all, related to the text of Genesis 1, whether it was a predictive timeline or something else. Again, both Paul and Isaiah are clear on this point.

It turns out, the precise timing of Christ's arrival was *not* predicted by the rabbi's 7000 year theory, but rather by God Himself, in the 70 weeks prophecy of Daniel 9. The interpretation of Daniel's prophecy was not hidden by God, unlike the spiritual mystery of Genesis 1, and indeed it was very well known to the Jews even before the advent of Christ.

> Regarding the times referred to in Daniel's prophecy, Rabbi Judah, the main compiler of the Talmud, said, 'These times were over long ago', Babylonian Talmud Sanhedrin 98b and 97a.
>
> In the twelfth century A.D., Rabbi Moses Ben Maimon (Maimonides), one of the most respected rabbis in history, and a man who rejected the messianic claims of Jesus of Nazereth, said regarding Daniel's seventy weeks of prophecy: 'Daniel has elucidated to us the knowledge of the end times. However, since they are secret, the wise [rabbis] have barred the calculation of the days of Messiah's coming so that the untutored populace will not be led astray when they see that the End Times have already come but there is no sign of the Messiah' [Igeret Teiman, Chapter 3, p. 24.]

Finally, Rabbi Moses Abraham Levi said regarding the time of Messiah's coming: 'I have examined and searched all the Holy Scriptures and have not found the time for the coming of Messiah clearly fixed, except in the words of Gabriel to the prophet Daniel, which are written in the 9th chapter of the prophecy Daniel.' [The Messiah of the Targums, Talmuds and Rabbinical Writers, 1971]

In the Targum of the prophets, in Tractate Megillah 3a, which was composed by Rabbi Jonathan ben Uzziel, we read: 'And the (voice from heaven) came forth and exclaimed, who is he that has revealed my secrets to mankind?.. He further sought to reveal by a Targum the inner meaning of the Hagiographa (a portion of scripture which includes Daniel), but a voice from heaven went forth and said, enough! What was the reason?--because the date of the Messiah was foretold in it!' In this amazing commentary from the Targum of the Prophets, the writer expressed the knowledge that Daniel's prophecy referred to the coming of the Messiah.

Furthermore, it is well established that the Jews of the Qumran community (the writers of the Dead Sea Scrolls) believed that Daniel's seventy weeks prophecy pinpointed the time of the coming of the Messiah. In fact, many in the Qumran community based their Messianic hope on similar chronological calculations. They believed that they were living in the generation to which this prophecy pointed![181]

Today this concept of a calculated 7000 year creation timeline is simply untenable, and dishonest with reality. It serves no spiritual purpose and sets the misguided expositor up for failure, as it has done for every one of its adherents across millennia. It encourages the activity of false prophets, who try to place maximum limits on the time of our Lord's return, and makes the Word of God seem foolish to those looking on. Any modern Christian who insists on maintaining a belief in the 7,000 year timeline, so called, must acknowledge the utterly speculative nature of the calculation,

---

[181] Mark Eastman, *The Search for the Messiah*, <https://www.blueletterbible.org/Comm/eastman_mark/messiah/sfm_06.cfm>.

grapple with its innumerable failures, and further admit the very source of the proposition. It does not originate from an explicit declaration within the Biblical text, but rather a mere assumption made by the spiritually blinded Jewish rabbis of the pre-Christian era.

And yet, the reader should be made aware. Although the 7000 year creation timeline calculations ultimately proved to be incorrect, the powerful testimony of Isaiah, and subsequently Paul, indicates that God did predict something, 'from the beginning' in His revealed creation text, with no reference to specific timing. The author asserts that Genesis 1 symbolically represents *what* would happen, and in what *order*, but not how long that process would take. In that sense, what we have is an orthodox position, stripped of its uninspired baggage. No Christian would imagine that God does not have an overall, predetermined plan for His creation. But we should be willing to identify and avoid scriptural inference, which only functions as a stumbling block. Further, we should be willing to investigate the spiritual meaning of the creation which is explicitly revealed.

IV.　What Is A Parable?

The Greek word παραβολή (parabolē), translated 'parable', is often assumed to refer to texts with a solely symbolic source, i.e. those texts that are based on events which did not literally occur. And yet, this narrow application of the term 'parable' is completely inaccurate.

When you think of the word 'parable', with respect to the Bible, the stories told by Jesus are usually the first to come to mind. Many of these stories did not literally occur, despite the fact that they were communicated in such a way as if they did occur, making use of common sense language and reasonable experiences. This explains perhaps why some readers may not like to refer to Genesis 1 as a parable. The common objection is that since the creation literally did occur, the text cannot be characterized as a parable.

But is this really a valid objection? Dictionary.com defines the English word 'parable' as 'a short, allegorical story designed to illustrate or teach some truth, religious principle, or moral lesson... a statement or comment that conveys a meaning indirectly by the use of comparison, analogy or the like.'[182]

The entry in Baker's Evangelical Dictionary is also enlightening.

> '**The range of meaning of the term 'parable' (Gk. parabole) in the New Testament closely parallels that of the Hebrew לְשָׁמ (mashal) in the Old Testament** and related Hebrew literature. As well as referring to narrative parables, the term identifies similitudes (Matt 13:33 ; B. Pes. 49a), allegories (Ezek 17:2 ; 24:3 ; Matthew 13:18 Matthew 13:24 Matthew 13:36), proverbs (Proverbs 1:1 Proverbs 1:6 ; Mark 3:23), riddles (Psalm 78:2 ; Mark 7:17), and symbols

---

[182] 'parable.' *Dictionary.com Unabridged.* Random House, Inc. 13 Dec. 2014. <Dictionary.com http://dictionary.reference.com/browse/parable> (13 Dec. 2014).

or types (Heb 9:9 ; B. Sanh. 92b). **'Parable' is a general term for a figurative saying.'**[183]

Smith's Bible Dictionary similarly states,

> 'As used in the Old Testament **it had a very wide application**, being applied sometimes to the shortest proverbs, (I Samuel 10:12 ; 24:13 ; 2 Chronicles 7:20) sometimes to dark prophetic utterances, (Numbers 23:7 Numbers 23:18 ; 24:3 ; Ezekiel 20:49) sometimes to enigmatic maxims, (Psalms 78:2 ; Proverbs 1:6) or metaphors expanded into a narrative. (Ezekiel 12:22) In the New Testament itself the word is used with a like latitude in (Matthew 24:32 ; Luke 4:23 ; Hebrews 9:9). **It was often used in a more restricted sense** to denote a short narrative under which some important truth is veiled. **Of this sort were the parables of Christ.'**[184]

The Holman Bible Dictionary more clearly explains a further distinction, which may explain the modern confusion surrounding the use of the term 'parable'.

> 'Parables utilize pictures such as metaphors or similes and frequently extend them into a brief story to make a point or disclosure. Nevertheless, **a parable is not synonymous with an allegory.**
>
> The difference between a parable and an allegory turns on the number of comparisons. A parable may convey other images and implications, **but it has only one main point established by a basic comparison or internal juxtaposition.** For example, the parable of the mustard seed (Mark 4:30-32;Matthew 13:31-32; Luke 13:18-19) compares or juxtaposes a microscopically small seed initially with a large bush eventually.
>
> **An allegory makes many comparisons through a kind of coded message.** It correlates two areas of discourse,

---

[183] Walter Elwell, 'Parable', *Baker's Evangelical Dictionary of Biblical Theology*, (Grand Rapids: Baker Book House Co., 1996). Emphasis mine.
[184] William Smith, 'Parable', *Smith's Bible Dictionary*, 17 May 2015. <http://www.biblestudytools.com/dictionaries/smiths-bible-dictionary/parable.html> (1901). Emphasis mine.

providing a series of pictures symbolizing a series of truths in another sphere. Each detail is a separate metaphor or what some call a cryptogram. If you are an insider who knows, you receive the second or intended message. Otherwise, you can follow only the surface story. Jonathan Swift's *Guilliver's Travels* is an allegory as is John Bunyan's *Pilgrim's Progress*. In the Old Testament, Ezekiel recounts an incident in nature about great eagles and vines (Ez 17:3-8) and then assigns a very allegorical application to each of the details (Ez 17:9-18).

The word allegory never appears in the Gospels. Parable is the basic figure Jesus used. Though no parable in the Synoptic Gospels is a pure allegory, some parables contain subordinated allegorical aspects, such as the parable of the wicked tenants (Mark 12:1-12; Matthew 21:36-46; Luke 20:9-19). ...

The Old Testament employs the broader category of mashal , which refers to all expressions that contain a comparison. A mashal can be a proverb (1 Samuel 10:12), a taunt (Micah 2:4), a dark riddle (Psalm 78:2), an allegory (Ezekiel 24:3-4), or a parable. The stories of Jesus are linked with the heritage of the prophetic parables in the Old Testament (Isaiah 28:23-29; Isaiah 5:1-7; 1 Kings 20:39-43; Ecclesiastes 9:13-16; 2 Samuel 12:1-4).[185]

Therefore, it is the differences in language and culture between the OT and NT that have contributed to the common misconception surrounding Biblical parables. Ancient writers were content to apply the word לְמָשָׁ (mashal) (MT) or παραβολή (parabolē) (LXX) in a sense that covers essentially all forms of literary comparison. Later NT writers, no doubt influenced by trends in literary culture, further subdivided these forms into more distinct categories. While Holman's Dictionary correctly makes the case for the distinction between parable and allegory in the NT, this distinction simply does not exist from the perspective of the OT where, for example, the

---

[185] Peter Rhea Jones, 'Parable', *Holman Bible Dictionary*, 5 June 2015. <http://www.studylight.org/dictionaries/hbd/view.cgi?n=4805> (1991). Emphasis mine.

'allegory' of Ezekiel 17 is referred to in the more generic sense as a מָשָׁל (mashal) (MT) or παραβολή (parabolē) (LXX.)

A brief analysis of these often overlooked examples of Biblical parables will demonstrate how we should better understand this literary genre. The prophet Baalam was inspired to communicate several לְמָשָׁ (mashal) (MT) or παραβολή (parabolē) (LXX) in the presence of Balak, king of Moab.[186] These were symbolic metaphors which illustrated his predictions of future, literal events. The aforementioned prophet Ezekiel also spoke a symbolic, and ultimately prophetic, לְמָשָׁ (mashal) (MT) or παραβολή (parabolē) (LXX) concerning the literal release of Israel from Babylonian captivity.[187] The author of Hebrews twice uses the word παραβολή (parabolē), usually translated in that instance as 'figure', to refer to the spiritual symbolism derived from literal OT events.[188] Jesus himself also indicated that spiritual lessons in parable format were to be derived from certain miracles that he had literally performed.[189] These examples stand alongside the more familiar Biblical use cases involving nondescript characters, and events that most certainly did not literally occur.

Thus, while it is of interest to evaluate the features and differences between various forms of literary comparison, there is absolutely nothing about the word 'parable' that requires it to be restricted to either literal or nonliteral events. The use of the word is irrespective of this distinction, and should carry no implication whatsoever regarding the factual occurrence of the events described. The sole requirement for a parable is that it employs a symbolic comparison, and there are indeed very many types of Biblical parables, as noted above. All Bible students should agree that parables teach important spiritual lessons, independent of their basis in reality, or lack thereof.

---

[186] Numbers 23:5-10, 16-24; 24:2-9, 14-25
[187] Ezekiel 17:1-24
[188] Hebrews 9:9; 11:19
[189] Mark 8:14-21

V.   He Created Them Male And Female

It is often suggested that the events of Genesis 1 and 2 overlap chronologically. One point put forth in favor of this view is that Jesus himself refers to the male and female from both creation texts in sequence. But this is not as straightforward as it might appear. In the first place, the presumed correspondence between the creation texts has presented many challenges to interpretation throughout history. In the second place, the teaching of Christ on marriage and divorce makes much more spiritual sense if the two texts are not forcibly merged.

Christ's words concerning marriage and divorce, with respect to the Genesis creation texts, are certainly worth our time to consider. [190] But the modern reader, being far removed from the historical controversy surrounding these texts, is at quite a disadvantage. Of course, the question posed to Christ by the Pharisees in the first century was intentionally controversial. But the reality is that Christ's appeal to the records of human creation, in response, was just as controversial. There is ample evidence to indicate that the two descriptions of human creation in Genesis did not easily lend themselves to unanimity of interpretation even at that time. History reveals that both Jews and Christians were forced to voice numerous and varied views which, nonetheless, did not undermine their sincere motive to better understand God's Word.

The Genesis Rabbah[191], for example, is a compilation of midrash or Jewish oral traditions that span several centuries before and after the first advent of Christ. It is an excellent witness to the problem of the male and female in creation. Of primary importance was the

---

[190] Matthew 19:3-12, Mark 10:2-10,
[191] H. Freedman and Maurice Simon, trans., *Midrash Rabbah*, (Soncino Press, London, 1961).
<https://archive.org/stream/RabbaGenesis/midrashrabbahgen027557mbp#page/n7/mode/2up>

need to understand why God appears to create humans together, in Genesis 1, but then appears to create them separately and in sequence, in Genesis 2. The Genesis Rabbah shows us that the rabbis were not in agreement on this matter.

Some rabbis reconciled the two creation texts by asserting that God first created Adam as a combination of both genders, and then subsequently split Eve off.

> 'And God said: Let us make man, etc. (i, 26).
> … R. Jeremiah b. Leazar said: When the Holy One, blessed be He, created Adam, **He created him an herma-**
> **phrodite** [bi-sexual], for it is said, **Male and female created He them and called their name Adam** (Gen. v, 2). R. Samuel b. Nahman said : When the Lord created Adam **He created him double-faced, then He split him and made him of two backs**, one back on this side and one back on the
> other side. To this it is objected: But it is written, And He took one of his ribs, etc. (Gen. 11, 21) ? [Mi-zalothaw
> means] one of his sides, replied he, as you read, And for the second side (zela') of the tabernacle, etc. (Ex. xxvi, 20).'[192]

> 'R. Hiyya b. Gomdi said : **He is also incomplete**, for it is written, And He blessed them, and **called their name Adam** - i.e. man (Gen. v, 2).'[193]

This conjoined character is often referred to in Jewish literature as the androgyne. [194]   For clarity, Dr. Freedman states that 'normally *androgynos* means one whose genitals are male and female; but here it means two bodies, male and female, joined together.'[195] 'Thus, **only both together are they man**.'[196] This is much different

---

[192] Rabbah VIII. 1. Emphasis mine.
[193] Rabbah XVII. 2. Emphasis mine.
[194] Ariela Pelaia, 'What Was The Androgyne? The Androgyne in the Biblical Story of Creation', < http://judaism.about.com/od/jewishculture/a/What-Was-The-Androgyne-Biblical-Creation-Story.htm> (26 Jan 2015).
[195] *Midrash Rabbah*, pg. 54.

than what we might assume from the plain text of Genesis 2, where the female is defined by virtue of the fact that she is 'taken out of man'. But according to these Jewish witnesses the female physically existed prior to the time when she was actually 'taken out'.

But there were other interpretations as well. Many rabbis believed that the female of Genesis 1 was completely distinct from the female of Genesis 2. Ancient witnesses tend to favor the suggestion that the first female was destroyed and recreated.

> 'R. Judah b. Rabbi said: **At first He created her for him** and he saw her full of discharge and blood; thereupon **He removed her from him and recreated her a second time**. Hence he said : **This time** she is bone of my bone.'[197]

> 'Cain rose up against his brother Abel, etc. Judah b. Rabbi said: **Their quarrel was about the first Eve**. Said R. Aibu: **The first Eve had returned to dust**.'[198]

The Book of Jubilees was a Jewish work widely cited by early Christian sources, and is dated conservatively to 200 BCE.[199] It describes another possible way to reconcile the creation accounts of male and female. Eve was thought to be created on the first week, but subsequently hidden from Adam until the second week.[200] Medieval Jewish sources introduced an even more outlandish alternative, whereby the first female became a demonic entity named Lilith and fled the Garden in response to her rival, Eve. [201]

> 'The Zohar (meaning "Splendor") is the Hebrew title for a fundamental kabbalistic tome, first compiled in Spain by Moses de Leon (1250–1305), using earlier sources. To the Kabbalists (members of the late medieval school

---

[196] *Midrash Rabbah*, pg. 133. Emphasis mine.
[197] Rabbah XVIII. 4. Emphasis mine.
[198] Rabbah XXII. 7. Emphasis mine.
[199] Wikipedia contributors. "Book of Jubilees." Wikipedia, The Free Encyclopedia. Wikipedia, The Free Encyclopedia, 24 Nov. 2015. Web. 21 Dec. 2015.
[200] Jubilees 3:4-8, <http://www.pseudepigrapha.com/jubilees/3.htm>
[201] Wikipedia contributors. 'Lilith.' *Wikipedia, The Free Encyclopedia.* Wikipedia, The Free Encyclopedia, 11 Jan. 2015. Web. 27 Jan. 2015.

of mystical thought), the Zohar's mystical and allegorical interpretations of the Torah are considered sacred. The Lilith of the Zohar depends on a rereading of Genesis 1:27 ("And God created man in His image, in the image of God He created him; male and female He created them"), and the interpretation of this passage in the Talmud. … the Zohar elaborates that the male and female were soon separated. The female portion of the human being was attached on the side, so God placed Adam in a deep slumber and "sawed her off from him and adorned her like a bride and brought her to him." This detached portion is "the original Lilith, who was with him [Adam] and who conceived from him" (Zohar 34b). **Another passage indicates that as soon as Eve is created and Lilith sees her rival clinging to Adam, Lilith flies away.**'[202]

So then why does God appear to create both male and female as distinct upfront? For some Jews, that's exactly what He did. For others, God simply altered His initial intent. For still others, God was looking ahead to the future. More severe blame was placed on Eve for her impending sin, and this was thought to explain the conflict.

'Then he paraded them [the animals] again before him in pairs, [male and female]. Said he, 'Everyone has a partner, yet I have none': thus, But for Adam there was not found a help meet for him! **And why did He not create her for him at the beginning**? Because the Holy One, blessed be He, **foresaw that he would bring charges against her**, therefore **He did not create her until he expressly demanded her**. But as soon as he did so, forthwith The Lord God caused a deep sleep to fall upon the man, and he slept (ii, 21).'[203]

The Babylonian Talmud contains oral tradition and commentary spanning a similar time period as that of the Midrash Rabbah. It reiterates several different opinions, including the one expressed above which foreshadows the evil inclination of Eve.

---

[202] Janet Howe Gaines, 'Lillith', Aug 11 2014, <http://www.biblicalarchaeology.org/daily/people-cultures-in-the-bible/people-in-the-bible/lilith/> (21 Dec 2015).
[203] Rabbah XVII. 9. Emphasis mine.

'R. Nahman b. R. Hisda expounded: What is meant by
the text, Then the Lord God formed [wa-yizer] man?
[The word wa-yizer] is written with two yods, **to show
that God created two inclinations, one good and the
other evil**....No difficulty arises for the one who says
that Eve was created from the face, **for so it is written,
wa-yizer, with two yods**....**For R. Abbahu contrasted
two texts**. It is written, 'Male and female created He
them', and it is also written, For in the image of God
made He man. How are these statements to be
reconciled? **At first the intention was to create two,
but in the end only one was created**. No difficulty
arises for him who says it was a face, since so it is
written, He closed up the place with flesh instead
thereof. ...'[204]

By contrast, the NT places more blame on Adam for sin because he
was 'not deceived'.[205]

But the Jewish methods of reconciling the plain texts of human
creation all seemed to contradict the fact that, in Genesis 1, both
male and female are equally created in the same image of God. This
means that even the proposed solutions above were, in a sense,
insufficient.

According to Rabbi Simlai, the meaning of creation in the image of
God was interpreted as applicable going forward, and did not apply
to the original state of man. This would eliminate conflict with
Genesis 2. He states 'man has already been made (cf . supra, 5 ad
fin .), and his seed shall henceforth be in our image, etc., as
explained in the text.'[206]

'R. Simlai said: Wherever you find a point [apparently]
supporting the heretics, you find the refutation at its side.
They asked him again: 'What is meant by, And God
said: Let us make man? 'Read what follows,' replied
he: 'not, "And gods created (wa-yibre'u) man" is written

---

[204] *Babylonian Talmud: Tractate Berakoth Folio 61a*, <http://www.come-and-hear.com/berakoth/berakoth_61.html>.

[205] I Timothy 2:14

[206] *Midrash Rabbah*, pg. 60.

here, but "And God created — wa-yibra" ' (Gen. 1, 27).
When
they went out his disciples said to him: 'Them you have
dismissed with a mere makeshift, but how will you
answer
us?' Said he to them: **'In the past Adam was created
from dust and Eve was created from Adam ; but
henceforth it shall be In our image, after our likeness**
(ib. 26) ; neither man without woman nor woman
without man, and neither of them without the Divine
Spirit.'[207]

'Philo of Alexandria, a Jewish scholar and philosopher living at the
time of Christ, 'shows an awareness of the problem in translating
'adam, and of its implications for identity, when he cites Genesis
2:16-17 (the first instance where the LXX translates 'adam with the
proper name Áääì):

> We must raise the question *what* Adam He commands
> and who is this; for the writer has not mentioned him
> before, but has named him now for the first time.
> Perchance, then, he means to give us the name of the
> man that was molded. 'Call him earth,' he says, for that
> is the meaning of 'Adam', so that when you hear the
> word 'Adam' you must make up your mind; **for the
> mind that was made after the image is not earthly but
> heavenly**.

Philo concludes that the scriptural redaction deliberately crafted and
made canny use of this ambiguity concerning identity.'[208]

Unlike their Jewish counterparts, early Christians did not speculate
regarding other women in the creation texts of Genesis, or
intermediate stages of physical human creation. But this did not
absolve them from all controversy. It merely required that they find
another way to circumvent the textual differences. As one might
expect, a uniquely 'Christian' solution began to take shape over the
course of several centuries, in the form of the doctrine of the

---

[207] Rabbah VIII. 9. Emphasis mine.
[208] Peter Bouteneff, *Beginnings: Ancient Christian Readings of the Biblical
Creation Narratives*, (Baker Academic, Grand Rapids MI, 2008), 29.
Emphasis mine

immortal soul. But as this doctrine took time to evolve, so too did the solution to the problem.

The second century Christian scholar Irenaeus came to a similar conclusion as Philo, when he identified the future application of the 'image and likeness' of man. He said 'what we had lost in Adam—namely, to be according to the image and likeness of God...we might recover in Christ Jesus.'[209] This of course would eliminate any physical application of the terms 'image and likeness', in the interim, and is one of the earliest documented Christian interpretations we have by which to understand the differences between the accounts of human creation. As the doctrine of the immortal soul was not a universal dogma of the church in his day, Irenaeus did not appeal to the soul as the basis for our understanding of God's image in us.

But by the third century, the doctrine of the immortal soul had begun more fully to emerge and so we find in the works of Origen a mixture of these sort of opinions on the matter.

> 'In some major texts, Origen distinguishes between the creation in Genesis 1:26-27 (which is an immaterial creation in the image) and the fashioning of Genesis 2:7 (where the body comes into existence). ...Yet Origen did not consistently teach that Genesis 1:26-27 referred to the creation and existence of bodiless human persons and that 2:7 referred to the addition of the body; his concept of the body itself ... is complex and variegated.'[210]

Into the fourth century, and beyond, the teaching of the immortal soul had been fixed within the church, and its utility with regard to understanding the creation of male and female was recognized. Basil of Caesarea 'discusses Genesis 2:7 and raises the question of how it relates to Genesis 1:26-27. He follows the teaching by some that the 'making' of Genesis 1:27 refers to the soul and the 'fashioning' of Genesis 2:7 refers to the body.'[211]

---

[209] Irenaeus, *Against Heresies* Book III Chapter XXVIII, <http://www.newadvent.org/fathers/0103318.htm>.
[210] Bouteneff, pg. 115.
[211] Bouteneff, pg. 147.

Gregory of Nyssa also wrote about this perspective, and yet clearly admits the uncertainty of the matter, as it has always been so.

> Gregory of Nyssa 'devotes the most attention to this matter in *On the Making of Humanity*, especially in the second half of the treatise... Before presenting his idea of the nature of human sex distinction, he says that ... 'we, as far as possible, **imagining the truth by guesses and images, do not expose that which comes to mind categorically, but will set it forth as in an exercise for those who consider charitably what they hear.**' ...
>
> What are these ideas that Gregory so cautiously proposes? They constitute nothing more than the consistent application of his lines of inquiry concerning the nature of the divine image and of the two stage creation.... Since there is no gender or sex in the God in whose image we were created, there must, in some sense or in some aspect of our creation, be no gender in us either... Aside from the logic of the argument alone, Gregory puts great stock in Genesis 1:26 as distinct from 1:27. At two points in *On the Making of Humanity*, he points out that the first verse, 'Let us make humankind in our image, according to our likeness' refers to a point where 'Adam yet was not,' for the reference here is to the humanity conceived by God. It is this 'universal nature' that is made purely in the image of God. The second passage (Genesis 1:27) refers to the temporal stage, where humans come into being...
>
> Gregory never fully resolves the tension between these views, and it seems that he knows it and thus clearly acknowledges the mystery of the underlying truth and the provisional nature of his speculation.'[212]

Now then, all of this confusion is not easily removed by the modern reader who presumes that the events of Genesis 2 are just details retroactively superimposed upon the sixth day of creation in Genesis 1. Such a simplistic assumption doesn't even address, let alone solve, the problems of interpretation which arise. While many ancient Jews and Christians did favor such a combined viewpoint in principle, the fact is that they could not all agree on how to make

---

[212] Bouteneff, pg. 168-170. Emphasis mine.

that viewpoint work in practice. Their persistent confusion is proof that the differences between the male and female of each text still exist, whether or not we force the extended human sequence back into the first creation week. But of course, the Bible does not actually tell us that the two creation texts in Genesis can be systematically reconciled. Rather, we find the earliest reference to this concept in the aforementioned Book of Jubilees, along with many other fanciful ideas.

We must now pause and reconsider the presumed simplicity of our modern perspective. If we are intent on using Christ's words about the creation of male and female, in the NT gospels, to somehow prove that Genesis 1 and 2 overlap chronologically, then we will inevitably miss the full significance of our Master's words. We will also stumble over the long and troubled history of interpretation that has come before us. We must first learn from Christ the lesson of male and female which he intends to teach, without superimposing our preconceived bias upon his exposition of the texts he quotes. Until and unless we do that, we are no better off than the 1st century Pharisees. We will have missed the point entirely.

Christ's juxtaposition of Genesis 1:27 with 2:24 does teach us that a relationship exists between the two passages. But the fact is that the two passages do not duplicate one another. By themselves, they do *not* teach the same thing, nor does one merely add detail to the other in a simplistic sort of way. Obviously, this is a matter for deep study. And we cannot fully understand this until we investigate the context of Christ's brief quotations. His excerpts are intended only as a point of reference.

The first quote, from Genesis 1, presents a simple statement of fact. 'He who created them from the beginning made them male and female'. The second quote, from Genesis 2, presents a commandment that derives from that simple statement of fact. 'Therefore a man shall leave his father and his mother and hold fast to his wife, and the two shall become one flesh'. Together, the two quotes convey a spiritual, and yet counterintuitive, principle. What Christ has done is call attention to the fact that God, by creating two different genders, actually intends for those two to be one.

But these two genders are by definition two. The irony of this is immediately plain, and its resultant difficulty has been well documented. Christ seizes upon this oddity of creation, and uses it teach the Pharisees about divorce. By selectively conjoining the two creation passages, Christ affects one with the other and perfectly illustrates first the spiritual ideal, followed by the physical reality. That is to say that he first condemns divorce in the general case, and then explicitly permits it in the special case.

Notice that 'in the beginning', that is Genesis 1, the method of human creation is not defined. Further, the 'male and female' have equal dominion and equivalent image. There is no prioritized order of creation between them, nor is the female taken from the male. They are created together. There is no explicit allusion to marriage, because theirs is a spiritual unity which has not yet been defined elsewhere in Scripture. There is no opportunity given to diverge from God's will. They simply obey God's commands. They are not restricted to Eden, but rule the earth in its entirety.

In Genesis 2, however, we find a much different circumstance. The method of creation of Eve from Adam initially portrays an element of division or separation. 'And the rib, which the LORD God had taken from man, made He a woman, and brought her unto the man'.[213]

> 'The first question to ask is whether the text suggests that Adam thought of Eve as having been built from his rib. The text gives us the answer: he did not. The first words out of his mouth were: 'This is now bone of my bones and flesh of my flesh' (Gen 2:23). **More than a rib is involved here** because she is not only 'bone of his bone' but also 'flesh of his flesh'.
>
> This leads us to ask then about the meaning of Genesis 2:21, NIV translates, 'He took one of the man's ribs and then closed up the place with flesh.' Adam's statement leads us to inquire whether the translation 'rib' is appropriate for the Hebrew word צֵלָע tsela'. The word is used about 40 times in the Hebrew Bible **but is not an anatomical term in any other passage**. Outside of Genesis 2, with the exception of II Samuel 16:13 (referring to the other side of the hill), the word is only

---

[213] Genesis 2:22

used architecturally in the tabernacle / temple passages (Ex 25-38; I Kings 6-7; Ezek 41). It can refer to planks or beams in these passages, but more often it refers to one side or the other, typically when there are two sides (rings along two sides of the ark; rooms on two sides of the temple; the north or south side; etc.). On the basis of Adam's statement, combined with these data on usage, we would have to conclude that God took one of Adam's sides-likely **meaning he cut Adam in half** and from one side built the woman.'[214]

This graphic representation of human creation by division does not sit well with the description of the male and female in Genesis 1, and attempts to force agreement require rampant speculation, as we have seen. Notwithstanding, the method of human creation by division cannot be overlooked. It cannot be reinterpreted as something other than what it plainly is. Without this element of division, the spiritual imagery is incomplete. And it can be illustrated in at least five different ways.

First, the creation of Eve from Adam does represent a method of division because it is explicitly dictated in the original text, as well as Christ's exposition of it. 'She shall be called Woman, *because she was taken out of man.*'[215] The term 'woman' requires division, and for this reason the female is not called 'woman' in Genesis 1. Christ confirms this method of division, when he concludes that *'they are no longer* two, but one flesh'.[216] Of course, that is to say that they were two beforehand. Eve became a distinct entity, with a distinct free will and opportunity for sin, despite sharing the same DNA so to speak.

Second, the creation of Eve from Adam does represent a method of division, because it proposes unity albeit with the future risk of divorce. The text says 'the man *shall*...hold fast to his wife'. That is what should be. But Jesus goes beyond that to assert that the commandment is only fulfilled in marriage. This by definition also teaches us the inverse. The commandment is not fulfilled when the

---

[214] John Walton, *The Lost World of Adam and Eve*, (InterVarsity Press, 2015), 76-77. Emphasis mine.
[215] Genesis 2:23
[216] Mark 10:8

unity of the two is broken. Divorce represents the final outworking of God's original division, or separation. The female and male consent to a union, and subsequently retract that consent. So they remain two different entities which God created to begin with. There should be nothing surprising about this observation. God accurately portrays every step of His spiritual process. This teaches us that all men and women are born separate from Christ as a result of sin. If they subsequently consent to a union with Christ, their separation is removed. If they do not honor the terms of their union, they are spiritually divorced from Christ. Although the initial separation and the final divorce are two different states, nevertheless the end result is the same.

Third, the creation of Eve from Adam does represent a method of division, because the given solution to that division, which is physical marriage, is temporary and will eventually be abandoned. This is found in the final exposition of Jesus on the matter. His closing remarks in Matthew 19 are often overlooked, as if they did not affect our understanding. 'The disciples [had] said to him, 'If such is the case of a man with his wife, it is better not to marry.' [Jesus] said to them, '*Not everyone can receive this saying*, but only those to whom it is given. For there are eunuchs who have been so from birth, and there are eunuchs who have been made eunuchs by men, and there are eunuchs who have made themselves eunuchs for the sake of the kingdom of heaven. *Let the one who is able to receive this receive it.*' Ultimately, Jesus answered the Pharisees' question by rendering the question irrelevant. He literally says that 'it is better not to marry' at all. He puts Genesis 2 in its place, and elevates Genesis 1, where there is no mention of marriage. The Pharisees' obsession with the legal limits of divorce betrayed their inability to recognize the long term inadequacies of marriage itself. The real spiritual message here is for the forgotten eunuch 'who is able to receive it'. So then the Scriptures clearly state elsewhere that physical marriage, in the resurrection, will be eliminated as inadequate and unnecessary.[217]

Fourth, the creation of Eve from Adam does represent a method of division because it is explicitly recounted in Paul's analysis of head coverings in the NT. He states 'For a man ought not to cover his

---

[217] Matthew 22:30, Mark 12:25, Luke 20:35

head, since he is the image and glory of God, but woman is the glory of man.'[218] No doubt the term 'image' itself is an echo of Genesis 1, nevertheless Paul's reasoning is not based on Genesis 1. Again, we find there that both the male and the female are equally created in the image of God and both are given dominion over all the creation. It is only in Genesis 2 that we find an element of division. Paul observes, 'for man was not made from woman, but woman from man. Neither was man created for woman, but woman for man.'[219] Therefore 'the symbol of authority on her head'[220], which is supported by Genesis 2, is undermined by Genesis 1. 'This mystery is profound, and I am saying that it refers to Christ and the church.'[221]

Fifth, the creation of Eve from Adam does represent a method of division, as an extension of the spiritual imagery defined by Paul. Notice the command once more from Genesis 2. 'Therefore *a man* shall leave his father and his mother.' Why is the command not given to the woman as well? It is because this man represents Christ, and he alone takes the initiative with his church. The church cannot 'leave' and 'hold fast' to him by her own will alone. This is an important spiritual feature which mirrors the marriage traditions of ancient culture. Similarly, the Pharisees asked Christ 'Is it lawful to divorce one's wife for any cause?' Why is the opportunity to initiate divorce not presumed for the woman as well? Again, the spiritual imagery requires this perspective. The man represents Christ, and 'He committed no sin, neither was deceit found in his mouth.'[222] He will never be unfaithful to his wife, which is the church. Only the church can be unfaithful to him, and so only he is eligible to initiate spiritual divorce.

So then division is an intentional part of God's creative process.

But how exactly can this division be overcome? Observe Jesus' statement to the Pharisees in Matthew 19. 'From the beginning it was not so'. What was not so? Is Jesus saying that 'from the beginning' divorce would not have been permitted under any

---

[218] I Corinthians 11:7
[219] I Corinthians 11:8-9
[220] I Corinthians 11:10
[221] Ephesians 5:32
[222] I Peter 2:22

circumstances, even in the case of adultery? Or, alternatively, is he saying that divorce as a concept did not exist 'from the beginning'? The difference between these two perspectives is vital, and we are forced to accept the later. Clearly, Jesus does permit divorce in the case of adultery, which proves that he does not deny all 'causes' outright. He thus only intends to teach us that divorce *should* not exist as per the beginning.

The semantic difference between *cannot* and *should not* is the key. If something should not be, it nevertheless may still be possible. We must carefully parse Christ's answers alongside the questions asked. The Pharisees were looking for divorce criteria, and we should not imagine that Christ responds with an example from creation that implies Divine prohibition of divorce. Rather, he responds with an example from creation that implies Divine disapproval of divorce. This is the obvious side effect of free will. The assumption that God initially prohibited divorce outright would force Moses into the uncomfortable position of altering God's true intention after the fact. But Moses received His instructions from God, and not the other way around. So then Genesis 2 must foreshadow a circumstance where divorce is theoretically possible, by virtue of the method of human creation by division. And yet God's distaste for divorce remains unchanged.

And the way to achieve unity, according to Christ, is to recognize the circumstances of the two genders back in Genesis 1. Unity is achieved through equality, cooperation, and obedience to God. The male and female of Genesis 1 are not bound by literal marriage and have no leeway to disregard God's command. Both dominion and image are conferred upon them, rather than legislated. Thus the method of human creation by division is not found in Genesis 1.

In other words, Genesis 2 does not accurately reflect the resurrection when 'they neither marry nor are given in marriage' in the physical sense. Genesis 1, on the other hand, does reflect the resurrection. It represents the spiritual ideal, which is a vision of the future that is never broken or altered. Until those spiritual conditions of the future are realized, however, it is God who subsequently creates by way of temporal division in Genesis 2. He knows the weakness of man and accounts for it by providing a path to spiritual restoration in the future.

This makes sense! 'Adam's humanity is a *provisional copy* of the real humanity that is in Christ.'[223]

> 'In 1:26 and 1:27a, it would be impossible to call 'adam a particular person, and certainly not a male person. This is why the LXX has here ἄνθρωπον and the NRSV says 'humankind'. In Genesis 2, where the provenance of female (iššа) from male (iš) is explicit and where the story tells of a particular man (and his mate), the Hebrew again refers to him as 'adam. Here too the LXX and all English translations-with the notable exceptions of the King James Version and New King James Version-use generic terms. They do not speak of a male (…). It is clear therefore that before there are male and female, 'adam does not refer to a particular male human being.'[224]

Putting all the pieces together, we realize now what Jesus has done. He has presented the nuanced differences between the two creation passages to the Pharisees, in order to undermine their legalistic perspective on divorce. First, the ideal case of unity between the anonymous genders in Genesis 1, apart from human marriage, renders their question about divorce spiritually moot. Second, Christ admits the weakness of flesh, and the risk of divorce, by highlighting the initial division between two specific, named persons in Genesis 2. And that is all before the sin in the garden! This theological dichotomy is ruined if the Genesis creations texts are forcibly merged. The 'image' of Genesis 1 should be kept far superior to the 'image' of Genesis 2. The incorporation of God's 'image' is a process, for both genders, that is not yet complete.[225] 'Just as we have borne the image of the man of dust, we shall also bear the image of the man of heaven.'[226]

---

[223] Karl Barth, *Christ and Adam: Man and Humanity in Romans 5*, (Collier, 1962), 46-47.
[224] Bouteneff, pg. 4.
[225] Romans 8:29, I Corinthians 15:49, II Corinthians 3:18, Colossians 3:10
[226] I Corinthians 15:47, 49

Printed in Great Britain
by Amazon